The Church Video Answerbook

THE CHURCH VIDEO ANSWERBOOK

R. CHIP TURNER

BROADMAN PRESS
Nashville, Tennessee

© Copyright 1986 • Broadman Press
All rights reserved
4237-13
ISBN: 0-8054-3713-4
Dewey Decimal Classification: 268.635
Subject Headings: VIDEO RECORDINGS // VIDEO TAPE RECORDERS
AND RECORDING // CABLE TELEVISION
Library of Congress Catalog Number: 85-24284
Printed in the United States of America

Library of Congress Cataloging-in-Publication Data

Turner, R. Chip, 1948-
   The church video answerbook.

   1. Television in religion. I. Title. II. Title:
Church video answer book.
BV656.3.T87   1986   254.3   85-24284
ISBN 0-8054-3713-4

Dedicated to my family—Sandy, Chris, and Cory—without whose patience and understanding this book would be but an unfulfilled dream.

A special word of appreciation is due my secretary, Sandra Williford, and my entire departmental staff for their support during this writing experience.

Contents

Introduction

1. Values of Video in My Church 13
2. Using Video in Religious Education and Other
   Church Programming 18
3. Using Cablecasting/Broadcasting in My Church's Ministry 33
4. Selecting Video Equipment for Religious Education
   and Church Programming................................ 38
5. Selecting Video Equipment for Use in Cablecasting/
   Broadcasting... 54

Appendix

A. How Video Works 62
B. Seventy-Five Programming Possibilities for Cablecasting/
   LPTV 68
C. One Hundred Uses of Video in Religious Education
   and Church Programming................................ 76
D. Checklist for Using Videotape in Religious Education 83
E. Video Equipment Maintenance Suggestions................... 84
F. Video Production Hints 87
G. Avoiding Copyright Infringements 97
H. Source Directory... 99
   1. Educational Video
      a. Religious Education Videotapes and Videodiscs 99

- b. Books on Using Video in Education and Religious Education 99
- c. Magazines on Using Video in Education and Religious Education 100
- d. Consumer Video Magazines. 100
- e. Professional Organizations for Educational Video Users ... 100

2. Cablecasting/Broadcasting
   - a. Religious/Family Television Networks 100
   - b. Books on Cablecasting/Broadcasting/LPTV/Satellite TV .. 101
   - c. Magazines on Cablecasting/Broadcasting/LPTV/ Satellite TV 101
   - d. Professional Organizations for Cablecasters/Broadcasters. 102

3. Personal Computers in Education
   - a. Educational Software. 102
   - b. Books on Personal Computers 102
   - c. Magazines on General and Church Use of Personal Computers in Education 102
   - d. Organizations for Users of Personal Computers in Religious Education. 102

4. Production Music Collections. 103

5. Manufacturers of Equipment
   - a. Audio Supplies/Microphones 103
   - b. Cameras 103
   - c. Camera Lenses. 104
   - d. Character Generators. 104
   - e. Editors (¾″) 104
   - f. Editors (½″ VHS). 104
   - g. Editors (½″ Beta). 104
   - h. Film Chain/Multiplexers. 104
   - i. Intercom Systems. 104
   - j. Lighting and Accessories. 105
   - k. Monitors. 105
   - l. Personal Computers. 105

  m. Prompting Equipment............................... 105
  n. Projection Video.................................... 105
  o. Satellite Receiving Systems 106
  p. Switchers and Special Effects Generators 106
  q. Test Equipment 106
  r. Time Base Correctors................................ 106
  s. Tripods and Dollies 106
  t. Videocassette Recorders (¾")........................ 107
  u. Videocassette Recorders (½" VHS) 107
  v. Videocassette Recorders (½" Beta) 107
  w. Videodisc Players (Laser)........................... 107
  x. Videotape Suppliers................................ 107
I. Video Glossary 109

Introduction

Writing a book on "basic video" seems to be "in vogue" today. There is no shortage of volumes dedicated to some facet of video usage or production. Yet, three concerns continue to surface as I consult each week with busy church leaders trying to incorporate video into their local church ministries:

(1) *Many available volumes labeled "basic video" actually mean a "basic engineering degree" is required to understand them!*

(2) *Purchasing video equipment of the right type and for a reasonable price can be frustrating in a rapidly changing environment. Claims of salespersons from fiercely competing dealerships punctuate the confusion.*

(3) *There is need for a reference piece which addresses the broad range of video possibilities for local churches. Concrete examples are sought for congregations of all sizes and in all locales.*

This book was conceived for local church leaders who are unable to find a single, concise volume to answer their ongoing inquiries.

Unique may be one of the best descriptive terms for the book's design. How many other books have you read which have a larger appendix than a body? Yet, the design corresponds to the book's purpose of providing easy-to-find answers to the expressed concerns:

(1) *"Basic" Information*—Every attempt has been made to make "basic" mean "simplified." The text is written in nontechnical terms. An extensive glossary provides additional basic information.

Step-by-step explanations are given whenever practical. Simple listings are scattered throughout the text. An appendix serves as a reference tool, offering detailed, targeted answers from "how to's" of video production to avoiding copyright infringements.

(2) *Equipment Selections*—Several types of video equipment are studied from videocassette recorders to satellite "dishes" . . . videodisc players to personal computers . . . television sets to connectors. Common features of each equipment type are shared to help you become an informed comparison shopper. The source directory in the appendix gives addresses to write for additional information on hardware, software, special interest organizations, and other resources.

An explanation of how video works underscores the significance of various equipment components.

We shall give attention to entry-level equipment for religious education applications. Another chapter addresses entry-level equipment for cablecasting or broadcasting with accompanying suggestions for building a complete video production package. There are even suggestions on how church leaders can take advantage of video without making *any* financial expenditures!

Simplified preventive maintenance techniques are explained to help protect your investment.

(3) *Video Possibilities*—A total of *175* realistic usages of video by the local church are to be found in the appendix. Each suggestion is followed by a word of explanation. One hundred of these suggestions are made for religious education and church programming applications. Seventy-five options are given for cablecasting as well as for low-power and full-power television broadcasting.

If you are seeking a "basic" reference volume on video for the local church, you have selected the right volume. You will not become an expert upon reading the book. You will, however, have a better understanding of how your church can benefit from using video in the ongoing ministry. And you will be able to lead other church members in video usage.

R. Chip Turner

1
Values of Video in My Church

"Why should I use video in my church?" If you are asking this question, you are not alone. Leaders of churches, both large and small, rural and urban, are making similar inquiries.

This chapter is designed to acquaint you with values of video for the local church as well as video limitations. Attention is given to broad applications from in-house religious education to cablecasting. Decreasing cost of video equipment and increasing outlets for video program usage no longer eliminate full video involvement by churches of all sizes.

Video is a tremendous tool for supporting the ongoing religious education, nurturing, and evangelism tasks of the church. In later chapters and the appendix, specific suggestions will be given for video usage within the church and its community.

If you understand the values of video for your church, you will likely want to become personally involved in using this supportive tool. Moreover, unrealistic expectations and pitfalls can be avoided as you understand video's limitations.

Among the values of video are:

Practical Substitute—Video creates the next best thing to personal contact between speaker and audience. Churches cannot always schedule or afford well-known teachers and speakers. Conversely, highly sought personalities are unable to be physically present every time and place where services are desired by local congregations. Videotapes of these same individuals allow churches greater flexibility in scheduling and budgeting while enlarging the person's ministry.

Immediate Feedback—There is no waiting for processing or depending upon a processor with video. Errors can be corrected quickly, and the quality of the production determined "on-the-spot."

Personal—Video is essentially a personal, intimate medium. Video can be used effectively on a small screen system such as a home television set.

Projection video has now advanced in quality and declined in price to make it practical for the average church. But, programming is most effective when the personality directs his remarks to the camera as if you were the only one viewer.

Economical—Videotape is inexpensive. For example, it is not uncommon to purchase a blank, two-hour VHS tape for less than the cost of one thirty-six-exposure roll of color slide film or a roll of home movie film. Unlike film, videotape may be reused many times. If material becomes outdated, you merely record new material onto the tape as you automatically remove the dated content.

Much video equipment is reasonably priced, too. Recorders and players for educational purposes are routinely sold for a few hundred dollars. This is in contrast to the thousands of dollars required just a few years ago. Even equipment for cablecasting is within the budgetary capability of most churches.

Efficient—Video can be produced and distributed in a short period of time, especially when compared to other visual media such as films and filmstrips. With careful preplanning, editing time is minimized or even eliminated in some cases.

Simple—Operation of most video equipment is simple. In addition, many church members are familiar with this equipment since they have video recorders in their homes. Operators are probably easy to find within your church membership.

Equipment for producing basic programs for cable television is also simple to operate. Use of home-type equipment is allowed by some small cable companies. Granted, operating hardware for more sophisticated productions requires advanced skills. Yet, you may be pleasantly surprised as you search for laypersons within the church with these abilities. If not, there are individuals willing to learn. Most churches have "grown" their workers as they have progressed in the breadth and complexity of their video ministries.

Reinforcement—The message can be repeated as many times as the viewer requires for reinforcing a learning goal. Using video in an individual or small-group setting, the learner has greater input into the learning process as he controls the video recorder.

Variable Record/Playback Speeds—For certain video equipment, recording can be done at various speeds. When high-quality reproduction is not required, slower recording speeds conserve videotape. Various playback speeds also allow for faster, slower, or even still-frame viewing for study of detail.

Editable—Videotape is edited electronically. Though highly sophisticated editing systems are costly, even the least expensive video recorders perform simple editing functions.

Easily Integrated with Other Media—Video integrates easily with other audiovisual sources such as motion pictures, slides, filmstrips, audiocassettes, and nonprojected visuals. If space and equipment availability are problems, all visuals for a teaching session can be converted to videotape. A videotape, video recorder and monitor, or television set replace all other equipment needed for the classroom presentation. (A simple video camera, recorder, and a blank wall for projecting the images are the only necessary components for transcribing other projectable media forms to videotape. Though a relatively expensive "film chain" is the ideal method of transfer, many well-equipped churches with broadcast television ministries use the blank wall, camera, and recorder approach. And, home-type units for transferring film to tape are now on the market for less than $50.) Video also supports a variety of teaching approaches from individual study to large group activities. By using a remote control, the teacher faces pupils at all times and maintains eye contact.

Learning Effectiveness—Experienced users of video in education have discovered that participants in sessions which include video as a teaching tool retain more lesson content. Participants also seem to enjoy the learning experience more.

Portable—Video equipment is becoming increasingly more portable and lightweight. Some recorders and small monitors are even packaged in briefcase-sized containers for easy transport. Since television sets are to be found almost everywhere, it is often unnecessary to carry a television receiver or monitor for events away from the church property.

Though cablecasting requires a higher quality of video equipment than some lightweight home models, modern cameras, recorders, and camera/recorder combinations are making production in the field much easier.

Time Shifting—Video allows for the taping of events at the viewer's convenience. Even if a church leader is unable to be present for a particular session, she can view the tape at a later time at the church or in her own home if she has a videocassette recorder.

Access to Homes—Increased security precautions are becoming commonplace in apartment complexes and planned communities. Visitors frequently encounter gates, guards, coded electronic entry systems, and other barriers. Personalized ministry to some individuals is difficult, if not impossible. Cablecasting offers access to these homes. Though not to be construed as a substitute for a personal visit, cable may, of necessity, constitute your first contact in some homes.

Educational videotapes also "open doors" for you. With a sizable percentage of homes equipped with video recorders, checking out tapes from the church media library for home use becomes feasible.

Audience Appeal—You are in the midst of the video age—instructional video, local cablecasting, personal computers, videodiscs, teleconferencing, and more. Local churches have the opportunity to do a better job of reaching and teaching people by using these video tools which have captured the attention of members and prospects. Video is here to stay. Wise church leaders ought to make positive use of this readily available resource.

Interactive Environment—Unlike many other audiovisual forms, video does not require a dimly lit room. Audience interaction is enhanced with greater light in a classroom. Learners are also able to see to take notes, thereby bolstering retention of subject matter.

With increased use of video, you will discover additional values to your own local church ministry.

Optimum use of video requires you to be aware of its limitations as well. Each of these limitations may be turned into a positive reinforcement:

Negative Mind-set—Some people have a mindset that television is a time waster. They do not take the medium seriously.

As it relates to educational video, programming must be carefully selected, properly introduced to learners, and followed up with appropriate teaching and learning activities. In other words, the video presentation is an integral part of the learning experience. It does not stand alone. For instance, if a teaching session is fifty-five minutes long, using a fifty-five-minute videotape is generally a poor use of the medium. There is no time for adequate introduction and follow-up.

As it relates to cablecasting, the burden of proving that a television program is worth the viewer's investment of time falls on the shoulders of the producer. If church leaders are not willing to spend their energy in planning and producing a worthwhile program, time will be wasted by viewer and producer. The larger test of a program's usefulness is not how much money you have invested in equipment. Rather, how well does the program meet the needs and interest of viewers? Providing quality Christian programming with audience appeal will overcome the negative mind-set.

Improper Expectations—People may expect to be entertained by television, not trained. Christian networks like ACTS Satellite Network, Inc., or CBN (The Christian Broadcasting Network) take positive advantage of this expectation to secure an audience and then impart Christian principles through religious dramas, musicals, magazine-format shows, and others.

Educational video, on the other hand, does not require an entertainment element to be effective. People will watch training tapes if they sense usefulness to them. Of course, there is no rule prohibiting an educational videotape from being entertaining to the viewer. And, you may actually increase content retention. (For instance, computer programs have successfully injected an entertainment flair to put the operator at ease and appear more "user friendly." This technique has not had an adverse effect on the learning outcome.)

Technical/Maintenance Requirements—Technical personnel and maintenance costs should be included in anticipated budget projections, especially for cablecasting purposes. Proper care and maintenance reduce the amount of repair expense. Moreover, video equipment is becoming simpler to operate and maintain.

Use of volunteers reduces or even eliminates personnel expense. Numerous churches involved in producing programs for cable or broadcast television have no paid personnel. Training for unskilled volunteers is now available in many areas through local cable companies, community cable channel access leadership and denominational agencies. Excellent video training tapes are readily available for loan or purchase from numerous video equipment manufacturers.

No Panacea—Television cannot do everything, nor does it replace existing media forms. You ought to recognize this fact if you are to make the best use of video.

In educational applications, video is merely another audiovisual resource to reinforce the teaching presentation. Properly used with adequate introduction and follow-up, video is one of the most effective resources for increasing participation and retention. Improperly used as a "time filler," video may actually impair the teaching process.

Illustration 1

FOUR VIDEOCASSETTE TYPES (clockwise from left corner): ¾″ U-matic, ½″ VHS, ½″ Beta, and 8 mm.

(Photo by R. Chip Turner)

Cablecasting does not replace the human touch. When programming is targeted to meet recognized needs and interests of people, no greater tool is at your disposal. Your people-reaching efforts will surely be strengthened when video is employed as a support mechanism. If used to replace personal contact with people, video will be a disappointment to you. Countless cases can be cited of churches launching major television campaigns to reach people without any accompanying personal contact. Predictably, these campaigns have been a disappointment to the leaders. Such campaigns have been an excellent means of introduction, needing personal contact and cultivation.

Not Interchangeable Formats—Video recorders are available in several formats, including 2", 1", 3/4", 1/2" VHS, 1/2" Beta, 1/4" and 8mm. (See illustration 1.) None of these formats is interchangeable with another. Similarly, videodisc formats are not interchangeable. Choosing a format with the greatest amount of software for your applications becomes most important.

The VHS (Video Home System) format is the most widely used for distribution of educational video. This 1/2" format—not to be confused with Beta which is also 1/2"—is also the choice of most home videocassette recorder owners. Your church's use of VHS for distribution makes it possible to send videotapes home for individual study.

Most producers of educational tapes choose the 3/4" format for making original tapes (masters). These 3/4" tapes copy better onto VHS tapes for mass distribution than copying VHS-to-VHS. Three-quarter-inch tape is also used by most church cablecasters. Though one-inch machines yield a superior master tape, cost of the equipment is significantly higher.

Small Picture Size—Television is "smaller than life" on most screens. With the quality of large screen and projection video units improving and the price decreasing as a result of marketing, this limitation is decreasing quickly. Churches can now purchase video projectors for little more than a 16mm movie projector.

Distractions—Television allows for distractions since it is not generally used in a darkened room. Moreover, viewers are accustomed to more freedom of movement in the home while watching television. For cablecasters, this means that an entire message must be conveyed in a short time frame. Network broadcasters design their programs to deliver a complete message in one segment between commercials—less than fifteen minutes! Though an entire program may be thirty minutes or an hour in length, messages must be delivered, and scenes changed several times within the program span.

For educational video producers, "brevity" is the watchword, too. A short tape or a longer tape designed to be stopped a few times for group activities will likely yield better results.

No Human Replacement—Television cannot take the place of a person. It is a tool to *support* teachers and leaders of church ministries and programs.

Limitations of video are few. They are usually related to a lack of preparation by the leader or a failure to understand video's role in the overall process.

Imagine how valuable video can be in your church's ministry. Read on! In the next two chapters you will be introduced to the "how to's" of video usage by the local church.

2
Using Video in Religious Education and Other Church Programming

Do you know church leaders who have delayed the use of video in their churches, thinking it to be futuristic? Have you been inclined to feel this way yourself?

The future is here! There is no better time to begin or enlarge video usage in your church than today. Besides the widespread availability of equipment at reasonable cost, video resources are plentiful and relatively inexpensive.

Consider these ten steps to utilization in your church:

First, discover the abundance of video material and technologies for individual use and class study.

Do-It-Yourself Tapes

One video source is your own church family. If the church owns a video camera and recorder, have teachers and learners create their own tapes. (Detailed suggestions on purchasing video equipment follow in a later chapter. Also, the appendix contains help in producing your own tapes.)

(An entire section in the appendix of this book details more than seventy ideas for such creative projects.)

Prerecorded Tapes

Another source of video material is prerecorded videotapes available from national, regional, and local denominational offices. Virtually every denomination has some involvement in video production. Or they have started libraries by purchasing from other sources.

For instance, the Southern Baptist Convention, through its state conventions, has funded a program called Video Tape Service (VTS). Various agencies of the denomination have provided programming for this cooperative effort. Local churches are able to purchase these videocassettes for little above actual tape cost, to borrow the tapes for a small service charge from a regional center or to borrow the tapes free from many state convention offices. Approximately two hundred titles are in the VTS collection, covering almost every aspect of church programming and religious education, pastoral ministry and personal development.

(Consult the appendix for a listing of several denominational and multidenominational sources of prerecorded videotapes. Most of these tapes are available on a free-loan basis or for a small fee.)

Rental of videotapes, whether from denominational suppliers, other religious producers or general producers, is a viable option. Literally thousands of titles on an almost endless array of topics are in libraries awaiting your request. These titles have been cleared for use in the type of situation you will be planning in the church. In other words, the rental library has received permission from the copyright holders to use the tapes in this manner.

[One tip: do not assume that tapes secured from a local store specializing in rental of movies for home use have been cleared for public performance. Ask first! Most of these tapes carry a notice at the beginning that they are "for home use only." Any other utilization may be a violation of the copyright law.]

When investigating sources of prerecorded tapes, remember to check with neighboring churches. Some leaders have amassed impressive libraries of useful tapes which they would be happy to share with others.

Satellite Educational Networks

Satellite networks dedicated to strengthening the local church are an additional videotape source. Several such networks are already in existence providing training and inspirational programs for church leaders and members. Some of these networks have been established by denominations while others are individual or church endeavors.

Two examples of nationwide denominational networks are the Catholic Telecommunications Network of America (CTNA) and Baptist Telecommunication Network (BTN).

State and regional denominational entities are also becoming involved in this educational networking. The Louisiana Conference of the United Methodist Church established such a network and regularly offers programming to its churches.

One example of a church establishing a satellite network is the Prestonwood Baptist Church of Dallas, Texas, founder of the Discovery Network Inc.

Given the variances in time zones and local church schedules, most programs on the nationwide denominational networks are designed to be videotaped for use at a time determined by the leader.

An idea of the variety and types of programming available on a satellite network for churches may be seen by this sampling of one month's schedule on Baptist Telecommunication Network as taken from the monthly *BTN Guide:*

> The following index lists this month's programs under areas of church work. Leaders should be aware that some topics such as "Media Library" may have programs related to other areas of work.
>
> Titles in italics indicate those programming messages that are being transmitted for the first time on BTN or contain new or revised material.
>
> Note that each listing provides approximate length . . .

BTN

Administering BTN in Your Church— Provides guidance for BTN coordinators on administrative details. (30 min.)

BTN: An Introduction— A brief explanation of the use of BTN in the local church. (15 min.)

How to Process BTN Messages— Guidance for preparing new BTN messages for use in the church and in cataloging permanent messages for future use. (15 min.)

What BTN Can Mean to Your Church— Presents ten ways BTN serves the local church as a denominational network. (15 min.)

The Work of the BTN Coordinator (15 min.)

Church Administration

Equipping Deacons as Servant Leaders— For use in deacons' meeting, the month's message focuses on ministering to families of the terminally ill. (30 min.)

The Pastor as an Overseer— Deals with the biblical and practical nature of pastoral leadership. "Overseer" is the true work of the pastor and must be biblically understood and applied for effective ministry. (30 min.)

Pastor Skills Series: Profile of a Small Church— First in a ten-part series designed for pastors of small churches, this segment deals with (1) primary vs. secondary relationships, (2) single-cell vs. multi-cell structure, (3) past vs. future orientation. (30 min.)

Church Building and Facilities

Improving Preschool and Children's Space (45 min.)

Improving the Worship Setting by Design (15 min.)

Church Training

Getting Ready for Children's Church Training— Helps for planning, conducting, and enriching each unit in *Exploring 1* and *Exploring 2.* (monthly/30 min.)

[*Exploring 1* and *Exploring 2* are curriculum pieces.]

Getting Ready for DiscipleLife Celebration— Help for coordinating youth choir, snack supper, worship, and fellowship around the Youth Church Training study theme. (monthly/30 min.)

How to Minister to New Church Members— Tells how to package a total program, from counseling to Christian Service. (30 min.)

Introducing Children's Bible Drill (20 min.)

Leading Preschoolers in Church Training (60 min.)

The LIFE Learning System—Introduces this new monthly series which provides support for leaders of Master Builder, an intensive course for multiplying leaders. Segments may be used in the group process. (30 min.)

MasterLife Discipleship Training—An overview of MasterLife with . . . testimonies. (30 min.)

MasterLife Focus—"Witnessing" will be the focus, featuring an interview . . . on the use of Continuing Witness Training and MasterLife, a demonstration of the Gospel in Hand presentation, and interview. (monthly/30 min.)

New Church Member Training for Older Children (60 min.)

Resource for Discipleship: Church Training Magazine—Presents a walk-through of the magazine for use by the Church Training Council. (monthly/15 min.)

Video Training Magazine (weekly/15 min.)
- "A Wednesday Evening Church Training"
- "A Sunday Afternoon Church Training"
- "Church Training by the Book"
- "An Overview of Curriculum"
- "Preparing to Lead Church Training Groups"

Family Ministry

Communication in the Christian Home (Part 1—30 min; Part 2—20 min.)

Dealing with Marital Conflicts—Gives valuable assistance in dealing with conflict in both marriage and the family. (45 min.)

Ministering to Families Today—Gives overview of this new monthly series, introduces the four areas of family ministry it will address, and provides orientation for the family life committee of a church. (monthly/30 min.)

Media Library

Resources for Vocational Guidance (15 min.)

Selecting Media for A Library—Two-part message giving guidance on selecting and evaluating books and audiovisuals, with special emphasis on media for children. (90 min.)

Missions

Acteens Making Meetings Work—Acteens leaders work with younger Acteens and older Acteens in separate segments to show how they organize the groups, plan the activities, and conduct the meetings. (30 min.)
[Acteens is a missions education organization for girls in grades 7 through 12.]

All Nations in God's Purpose—Presents what the Bible teaches about missions and how that teaching affects each of our lives. Study resources include a textbook and study guide titled *All Nations in God's Purpose: What the Bible Teaches About Missions*. (40 min. each)

The Laity Alive in Missions—Deals with involving men and boys in missions through prayer and an update on Baptist Men's Day. (25 min.)

Like a Mighty River—As drops of water become a mighty river, so scattered resources through the Cooperative Program become a powerful channel for Bold Mission Thrust. (30 min.)

The Missions Hour— Begins with a 5-minute feature each week titled "Missions File" which includes missionary profiles, mission news, and prayer requests. The following listing gives the titles of features which follow. A description of each title is given in this index.
- *(Missions Update, Acteens Making Meetings Work)*
- *(Like a Mighty River, MissionsUSA Video Magazine)*
- *(Profiles in Missions, The Laity Alive in Missions)*
- *(Missions Update, MissionsUSA Video Magazine)*

Missions Update—Features youth coffee house ministry in Austria, MISSIONS review, mass media ministry in Columbia. (25 min.)

MissionsUSA Video Magazine—This magazine features the first episode of "The Black Southern Baptist Church" with other segments featuring Hare Krishna and the chaplaincy. (30 min.)

MissionsUSA Video Magazine—Features part two of "The Black Southern Baptist Church"; . . . with street people; and Louisiana Southern Baptists reaching those who work on the oil rigs in the Gulf of Mexico. (30 min.)

Profiles in Missions—A series of five-minute segments portraying home missionaries at work. (25 min.)

Music

Introduction to Preschool and Children's Choirs—Introductory help on methods, materials, and concepts. (25 min.)

Introductory Helps for the Bivocational Music Leader and Music Director—Gives analysis of worship services and choir rehearsals and discusses various aspects of both. (30 min.)

Recreation/Drama

Recreation Helping a Church Accomplish Its Mission—Testimonies and practical ideas are given for utilizing areas of church recreation to assist a church in its ministry. (20 min.)

Special Ministries

Reaching Unchurched Persons by Home Bible Study—A preview of TeleGuide, an outreach plan in which church members employ the telephone and Home Bible Study Guide to reach unchurched persons. (25 min.)

Student Ministry

Evangelism with College Students—Focuses on evangelism on the beach. (monthly/30 min.)

Involving Students in BSU (2 hrs.)

[BSU—Baptist Student Union—is a ministry to college students.]

Student Ministry Pro Files—Talks with a pastor about pastoral ministry to students. (monthly/30 min.)

Sunday School

Bible Book Preparation for Adult Sunday School Workers (weekly/20 min.)

Bible Book Preparation for Youth Sunday School Workers (weekly/20 min.)

[*Bible Book* is a curriculum line for youth and adults.]

Convention Uniform Series Preparation for Adult Sunday School Workers (weekly/20 min.)

Convention Uniform Series for Youth Sunday School Workers (weekly/20 min.)

[*Convention Uniform* is a curriculum line for youth and adults that follows the International Sunday School lessons' Scripture suggestions.]

Decalogue for Prospects—Ten plans to increase a church's prospect file. (30 min.)

Department Directing in Adult Sunday School Work, Parts 1-5 (45 min. each)

Developing Skills in Biblical Interpretation (50 min.)

Growth through Vacation Bible School—Identifies five kinds of growth that can occur through VBS. (25 min.)

How to Find Prospects within the "Four Walls" (30 min.)

How to Start a Dual Sunday School (30 min.)

Introducing College Concern—A detailed description of the College Concern Emphasis which calls churches to action in reaching more college students for Bible study and strengthening the church's ministry to students away. (30 min.)

Introduction to the Weekly Workers' Meeting Messages for Youth Sunday School (15 min.)

Life and Work Preparation for Adult Sunday School Workers (weekly/20 min.)

Life and Work Preparation for Youth Sunday School Workers (weekly/20 min.)

[*Life and Work* is a curriculum line for youth and adults.]

The Pastor Leading the Sunday School in Growth (20 min.)

Sunday School—An Avenue for Witnessing—Describes and illustrates how the Sunday School supports personal witnessing. (15 min.)

Sunday School Administration for Youth Workers, Parts 1 to 4
- "Developing Administrative Skills" (60 min.)
- "Developing Leadership Skills" (60 min.)
- "Developing Reaching/Witnessing/Ministering Skills" (60 min.)
- "Developing Teaching/Learning Skills" (2 hrs.)

VBS: A Reaching and Teaching Experience—Reviews the history and development of VBS work, including the present Southern Baptist Convention training plan and materials available. (60 min.)

General

Aids to Estate Planning—Acquaints the viewer with vital information on estate planning and how the Baptist Foundation can help an individual's Christian witness live on after death. (20 min.)

Developing Skills in Telling Bible Stories to Children (30 min.)

Educating Tomorrow's Leaders: The Role of Baptist Colleges and Schools—An overview of Southern Baptist educational institutions' purpose and commitment to Christian education. (30 min.)

Getting Ready for Youth Week—Assists youth and adults in preparing for Youth Week. (60 min.)

God's Unfinished Dream: 125 Years Southern Seminary—Southern Baptist Theological Seminary celebrates its 125th anniversary. (30 min.)

Introducing New Orleans Baptist Theological Seminary (30 min.)

Liberty Under Christ, Episode IV—A segment of the six-part series: Meet Southern Baptists. An additional resource to accompany this programming is the Baptist Heritage Series of pamphlets, available from the Historical Commission of the Southern Baptist Convention.

SBC NewScene—News and features from denominational agencies and institutions. (weekly—15 min.—repeated same day at 2:00)

The Southern Baptist Convention: My Church at Work Around the World—Explains how the SBC is structured and how its boards, commissions, and institutions work together to carry out the Great Commission. Some key leaders of the denomination are featured. (25 min.)

Southwestern News—Informational features for the local church from Southwestern Baptist Theological Seminary (15 min.)

Permission is granted to BTN subscribers to duplicate copies of *BTN Guide* for their use.

BTN Guide is a publication of the Sunday School Board of the Southern Baptist Convention, 127 Ninth Avenue, North, Nashville, Tennessee 37234. Lloyd Elder, President; James W. Clark, Executive Vice-President.

BTN Guide is mailed each month to subscribers to BTN, a satellite telecommunication network owned and operated by the Sunday School Board to provide information, inspiration, and educational assistance to the local church.

For more information, call or write: BTN, 127 Ninth Avenue, North, Nashville, TN 37234.

For each program it produces, BTN provides a utilization guide for teachers and leaders. The guide offers suggestions for proper introduction and follow-up as well as other learning reinforcement activities. [End of *BTN Guide*]

Churches wishing to participate in a satellite network must have access to a satellite receiving system ("dish"). Such a receiving system is within the financial capability of most churches. Some denominations even have purchase plans whereby a church can secure the needed equipment on a time payment plan at reasonable interest rates.

Some churches may have access to satellite signals through the dish of a church member.

A videocassette recorder with a tuner/timer is useful since this machine can be set to record a program unattended.

Video Teleconferencing

Besides original production, prerecorded videotapes and satellite-delivered material, video teleconferencing is an additional source which adds spontaneity to the learning process. Teleconferencing exposes the learners to an outstanding leader or leaders in another location without some of the time and expense restraints. Five types of video teleconferencing, ranging from very inexpensive to expensive, are:

Tape—Phone

This teleconference method features the showing of a prerecorded videotape provided by the guest leader. (See illustration 2.) After the class has viewed the tape, a live, two-way telephone conversation takes place between the guests and the learners. Since no video transmission equipment is required, the cost is minimal.

Slow Scan—Phone

Use of a live, slow scan television image of the guest leader making his presentation is the basic feature of the teleconferencing technique. (See illustration 3.) Learners still respond via telephone lines. (Slow scan television is like looking at a series of slides rather than full broadcast video.) Since slow scan television is sent over telephone lines, no satellite or broadcasting entity is necessary. Though this television imaging is slightly

TELECONFERENCING

GUEST SPEAKER   LEARNERS

1. Tape—Phone
Illustration 2

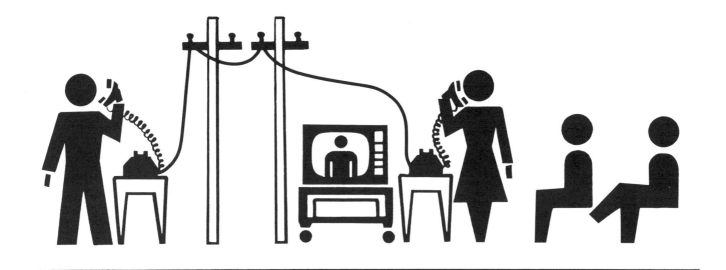

2. Slow-Scan—Phone
Illustration 3

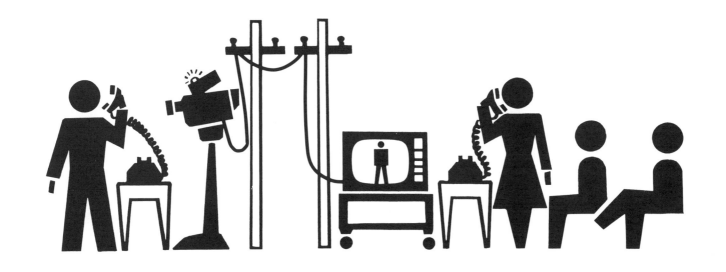

less effective than full video, the cost is significantly less. Also, enough changes in the picture take place to observe reactions by the leader. Special video equipment, possibly available through the telephone company, is required at the leader's end of the teleconferencing setup.

Slow Scan—Slow Scan

This teleconferencing method employs slow scan video at each end. (See illustration 4.) Though there is obvious value to the leader being able to see participants, the cost is increased significantly.

Full Video—Phone

By using full video pickup capabilities to televise the guest leader, participants see him as he would appear on a regular television program—"live and in color!" (See illustration 5.) Response by learners is still via regular telephone lines. Until recently, this teleconferencing method was extremely costly. However, with the proliferation of new networks which have available time for rent on their satellites and the availability of uplinking (sending a signal up to a satellite) facilities, full video—phone becomes realistic in many cases.

For instance the first video—phone teleconference on Baptist Telecommunication Network enabled viewers nationwide to hear live reports by key denominational leaders on the growth of foreign missions. Participants were then invited to ask questions by telephone. Since the satellite transmission equipment was already in place, the satellite transponder time was owned by the network, and the satellite receiving locations were those of current BTN subscribers, the teleconference was very cost effective.

Full Video—Full Video

In this teleconference approach, both guest leaders and learners see and hear each other on live television. (See illustration 6.) This is the most costly method and the least convenient. Not only is the leader required to go to an uplink site, but the learners must also do so or rent a portable uplink. As with other video technology, however, costs are decreasing with progress. Some situations justify such an expense.

One relatively low-cost application of full video—full video is an in-town teleconference if your area has two-way capabilities. If so, learners from numerous locations throughout the cable coverage area can interact with a leader via cable.

Interactive Video

Still another source of video for religious education and church programming is interactive video. This technique allows a learner or learners to secure responses from video equipment in a planned sequential approach. There are at least three possible methods of interactive video available to you:

Computer Only

By using a small personal computer, a video screen, and a computer disk drive, a learner is able to get help on a variety of topics including Bible-related ones. A participant's response determines the progress he makes in the learning experience.

Many professionally produced, biblically based programs are already being marketed for such usage. One example of such a computer program with sizable benefit to ministers and laypersons is *The Word Processor*. This multidisk program with editions for several brands of personal computers enables learners to do biblical word studies, topical studies, and more. Among its features is an extensive concordance. Bible researchers are able to do far more and more quickly than with less interactive methods.

Amateur computer programmers are producing hundreds of other biblically based programs which are shared with friends and members of computer clubs nationwide. These programs are being created by pastors, church staff members, and laypersons. If you cannot find such programs, just ask any computer enthusiast.

(See the source directory in appendix for a listing of some nationwide religious computer organizations.)

Computer—Video Recorder/Videodisc

When the personal computer is linked to a stor-

3. Slow-Scan—Slow-Scan

Illustration 4

4. Full Video—Phone

Illustration 5

5. Full Video—Full Video

Illustration 6

age device such as a video recorder or a videodisc player, high resolution pictures are included in the interactive process. Learners not only read about a topic; they are able to see it fully visualized. Laserdiscs (videodisc players which use a laser beam to "read" disk information) are especially adaptable to interactive video. Each frame of the thousands of such frames on a disc has an identification number which enables instant access. Correct answers will take the learner to another predetermined frame for an additional learning experience. Incorrect answers require the user to review, gain additional background information, and then progress.

Cable—Cable

In areas which have interactive cable, learners are able to access the database established by a cable system. Though there may be some religious education material, a more likely value is for churches with schools. Pupils access the database for doing a variety of research, thus expanding library capability without adding more in-house materials.

Teletext

An additional source of video information deserves brief mention since it has the potential for supporting religious education and church programming. Teletext is a method of distributing printed information without paper. "Pages" of information are coded onto a television signal and sent out by regular broadcast stations, cable systems, or satellites.

Users—individuals or churches—must have a decoder to receive this information. Textual information is sent on the same channels as regular television but does not interfere with quality of reception of existing programs. This approach is already used by major television networks in providing captioned programming for the hearing-impaired. Some retailers use teletext for making their catalogs available to in-home shoppers. Shoppers select merchandise and place orders from the easy chair in the den!

Since several religious education networks targeted to the local church are already in existence (as mentioned earlier), religious cable channels are becoming commonplace, and religious/family networks aimed toward the homes are flourishing (see the next chapter); teletext becomes an increasingly realistic source of video-delivered information for support of religious education and church programming. Churches with schools can already benefit from research data via teletext.

As denominational entities and producers of religious material employ teletext distribution, Bible students can do research at home or at church; ministers can access the latest information available on programs, plans, theological thought, sermon preparation, and so on.

Teletext also may be used eventually for delivering curriculum material and other data to churches or regional printing centers. Costs for shipping would be reduced significantly while delivery time would be virtually instantaneous. (Many secular publishers are already using similar technology for textual distribution.)

Second, once you are aware of the extensive variety of available video sources and technologies, make selections based on the learning goals for a teaching session. (Even if the usage being made of video is not in a formal teaching session, there should still be some goals, objectives, or expected outcomes for the session.)

Among the most affirming contributions you can make to proper use of video in your church is to underscore video's supportive role to the teacher or leader. A videotape should *never* be used to fill time. If a tape's content does not undergird the purpose for the meeting, do not use it. If the reason for the meeting is simply to show a tape without proper introduction and follow-up, avoid having the meeting!

Third, secure the video playback equipment and videotape(s). With the increasing popularity of video usage, do not assume the equipment is available. In many cases videocassette recorders or players, television sets or monitors, and rolling carts may be reserved in the church media library (church library).

The library is frequently a source of videotapes and/or catalogs listing accessible videotapes. If the church subscribes to a satellite-delivered service like BTN, the library is a suggested location for receiving, recording, and distributing the video material and utilization guides. The librarian may also be familiar with nearby denominational video outlets.

If the selected videotape is from a distant source, allow plenty of time for shipment. Tapes are often shipped at a far less expensive library rate and may require extra delivery time.

Fourth, preview the video material. Take notes about content, possible materials needed to follow up the video message, and length of the program. Determine whether it would be better to use the entire tape or only selected portions. Carefully study any accompanying supportive materials. By ordering a videotape well in advance, you will be able to have more preview time. And, in the unlikely event that you receive a damaged tape, there will be time to secure a replacement. Similarly, mechanical problems with playback equipment can be identified and repaired well in advance of the projected use date.

Fifth, plan for the video presentation to be an integral part of the teaching plan. A videotape is simply another audiovisual teaching tool. Though viewing of a tape may be a highlight, the focal point of the session should be the leader who guides learners toward accomplishing predetermined goals.

Sixth, arrange the classroom environment for optimum viewing and comfort. (See illustration 7.) Chairs should be placed so that participants view the television screen as close to "head on" as possible. Viewers begin noticing distortion when they are angled greater than thirty degrees from the frontal position. Placing the television set in a corner with chairs arranged in front in radiating semicircles is best. Tables may be added if desired by the leader.

Ideally, the most distant viewer should be no more than approximately six times the measurement of the television screen. Otherwise, diagrams and letters are difficult to see.

(For instance, if you are using a 25″ television screen, the most distant viewer should be no more than 12.5′ away: 6 × 25″ = 150″ ÷ 12 = 12.5′. If larger screens are not available to satisfy this formula, join multiple television sets together with cables and a signal splitter.) (See illustration 8.)

The television set or monitor should be four to six feet above the floor and tilted slightly forward to avoid glare. Also, do not place the set near windows or other bright light sources. To do so will cause discomfort for viewers looking into the bright lights.

Unlike some other audiovisuals, it will not be necessary to darken the room for video. Learners may wish to take notes and will have difficulty doing so in a darkened room. To optimize attention spans, be certain that room temperature is comfortable, certainly not warm.

Seventh, connect all video components prior to the class session. This will allow time for replacement of defective connectors or to secure help if there is any confusion regarding proper connection of the recorder or player to the television set or monitor. (See illustrations 9 and 10.)

Eighth, conduct the learning session, properly introducing video material at the appropriate time and following up the viewing with appropriate reinforcement activities. If there is no time for introduction and follow-up, avoid using the tape.

Ninth, return the equipment and videotape. If appropriate, disconnect the video components. Report any equipment problems to avoid future disappointment by users.

When a tape must be mailed back to a library or rental agency, do so promptly. Delays may cause someone else to miss a future viewing.

Tenth, evaluate the entire teaching session, including the effectiveness of the video presentation. Make notes for later reference and to share with other leaders as appropriate.

Used properly, video is one of the best tools available to church leaders for religious education and church programming support. Video is familiar and appealing to viewers; it increases learning retention; the equipment is easy to use, the cost is affordable, and both hardware and software are widely available.

Note

1. *BTN Guide* is a publication of Baptist Sunday School Board, 127 Ninth Avenue, North, Nashville, TN 37234.

TYPICAL EDUCATIONAL VIEWING SETUP

Illustration 7

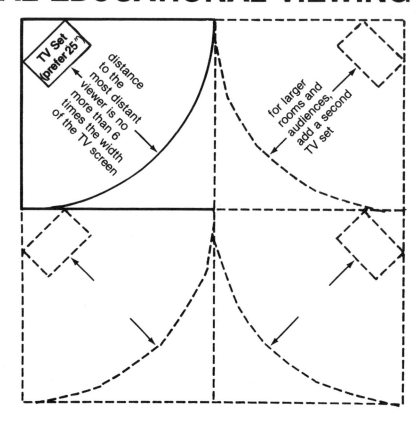

Connecting One Videocassette Recorder or Video Player to Multiple Receivers (Television Sets)

Illustration 8

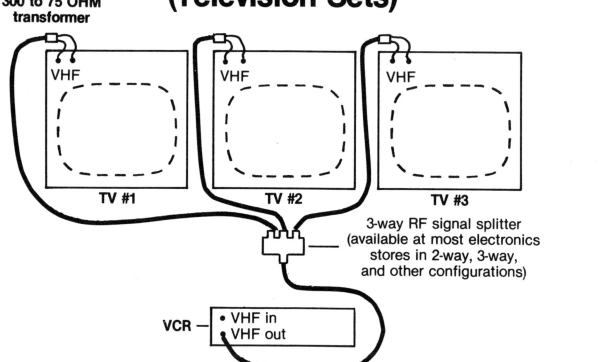

SOME TYPICAL VCR HOOKUPS

Illustration 9

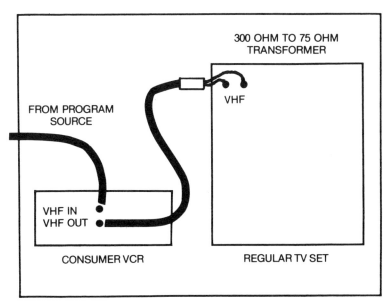

1. Connecting a consumer-type VCR to a regular television set.

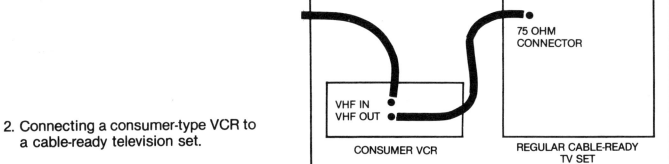

2. Connecting a consumer-type VCR to a cable-ready television set.

Illustration 9 Continued

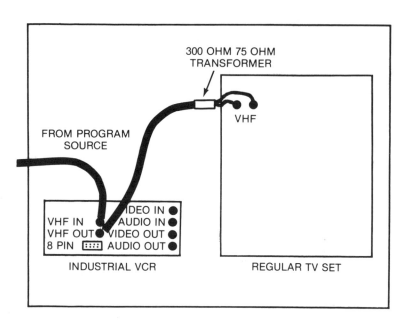

3. Connecting an industrial-type VCR to a television set using a single coaxial cable with F-type connectors to go from "VHF out" of the VCR to "VHF" of the TV.

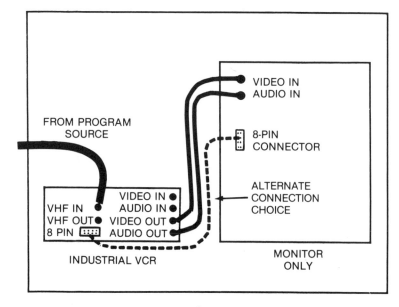

4. Connecting an industrial-type VCR to a monitor by either of two methods: (1) using cables to connect "video out" of VCR to "video in" on monitor and "audio out" of VCR to "audio in" on monitor or (2) using an eight-pin connector cable between VCR and monitor.

Illustration 9 Continued

5. Connecting a consumer-type VCR to a monitor/TV using a single coaxial cable with F-type connectors to go from "VHF out" of the VCR to "VHF" of the monitor/TV.

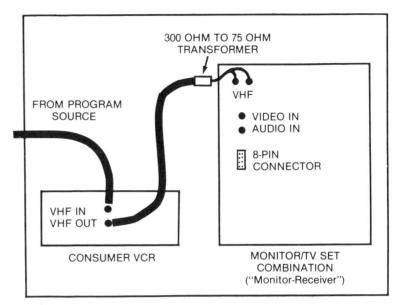

6. Connecting an industrial-type VCR to a monitor/regular television set combination by using any one of three methods: (1) using a single coaxial cable with F-type connectors to go from "VHF out" of VCR to "VHF" of monitor/TV, (2) using two cables to connect "video out" and "audio out" of VCR to "video in" and "audio in" on monitor/TV, or (3) using an eight-pin connector cable between VCR and monitor/TV set.

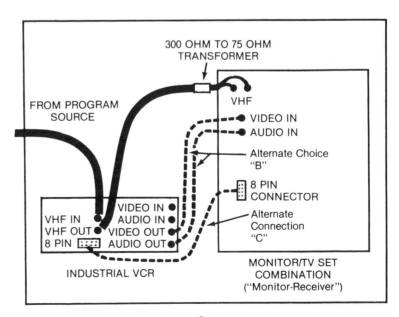

Illustration 9 Continued

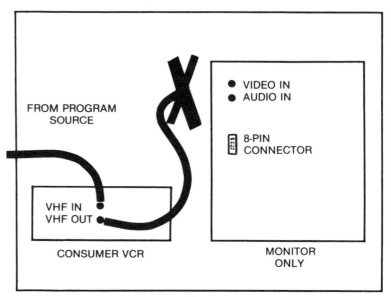

7. Illustration shows that if you choose a consumer-type VCR, it will not likely connect to a monitor only since the VCR will not have "video out" and "audio out" or an eight-pin outlet.

**7
(INCOMPATIBLE)**

VCR HOOKUP FOR DUBBING (DUBLICATING) VIDEOTAPES

Illustration 10

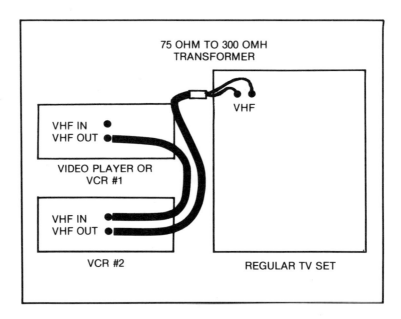

The simplest method when using two VCRs or a player and a VCR is to go from "VHF out" of the source machine to "VHF in" of the copying recorder. If the source machine has "video out" and "audio out" connections and the copying recorder has "video in" and "audio in," two cables may be used to connect audio to audio and video to video as an alternate dubbing method.

3
Using Cablecasting/Broadcasting in My Church's Ministry

"We may be small, but we don't have to think small!" Those were the pastor's words when I asked him about the presence of television cameras in the church sanctuary. And he was absolutely correct in his response. Though the church was *small* in membership, the budget was *small,* and the community was *small,* the pastor and his people were *big* thinkers! With two borrowed, home-type video cameras, virtually no funding, and all volunteer workers, the church was producing a weekly television program. This program reached into the homes of more people than would fill their sanctuary several times over.

Churches have been involved in broadcasting for a long time. Yet, the number of churches on television has been severely limited by high costs and availability of space on existing stations. Deregulation of broadcasters by the federal government has brought additional complications. Churches have frequently found it impossible to retain their purchased time slots at any price, being pushed aside for more lucrative programs such as professional sports.

Churches unable to secure a regular time slot on broadcast television found the purchase of spot announcements to be an expensive alternative. In some of the largest television markets, a single, prime-time spot costs from several hundred dollars to a few thousand dollars.

As the "small" church with the "big" ideas learned, however, the era of religious communication has now opened to churches of all sizes, in most locations, and in most financial circumstances. This era has been sparked by the rapid growth of cable television and the promises of a new communications medium: low-power television (LPTV). Churches have learned air time is available at low cost, often even free. Video equipment prices have continued to drop. In some circumstances, equipment has been made available on a free loan basis.

Cable Television's Audience Potential

Use of cable television to deliver the church's message has been dismissed by some as being ineffective due to a limited audience. While such a feeling may have had validity in the early days of cable, this is no longer true. Consider these facts:

1. Of the more than 85 million homes with at least one television set—almost every home in America—approximately 70 percent of them are already passed by cable television lines[1] and the number is growing rapidly.

2. Over 35 percent of America's households are already subscribers to cable television with this number expected to be over 50 percent by 1990. More than 30 percent will be subscribing to additional tiers of service in 1990.[2]

3. Cable, low-power television, independent stations, public television, and other outlets are already significantly impacting the viewership of the three major networks. The networks' share of audience-watching television dropped below 80 percent for the first time in 1984. This drop was even more significant since it represented a loss of nearly 4 percent from the previous year.[3]

4. By 1990, the estimated networks' share of audience in all television households is anticipated to be only 65 percent.[4] In the mid 1980s, the networks' share in cable households already stood at only 64 percent.[5]

5. People are watching television. Over fifty hours are viewed in the average television house-

33

hold with over three hours of this being cable originated programming.[6]

6. In many smaller communities, more than 60 percent of the households are already cable subscribers.[7] This percentage is growing in large metropolitan areas, too, where cable has only been allowed for the past few years.

As can be seen, cable television has the potential of delivering a sizable audience to the local church which produces programming to meet the needs and interests of people in the community.

Cable's Current Programming Lineup

Cable television is now offering programming to subscribers never before thought possible because of time restrictions on major network affiliates. New cable systems and those being upgraded are offering in excess of thirty channels, some even beyond one hundred channels with an enormous spectrum of programming.

A number of networks with a mix of family and religious programming are available to the cable operator. A few examples are:

ACTS Satellite Network, Inc.
Christian Broadcasting Network (CBN)
Eternal Word Television Network (EWTN)
National Christian Network (NCN)
People that Love Network (PTL)
Trinity Broadcasting Network (TBN)

Some of these networks may be preempted to provide local programming. The ACTS network encourages churches to produce local programming by setting aside several hours each day for local origination, plus four minutes every hour—twenty-four hours per day—for local insertions. One of the insertions is a two-and-a-half-minute slot, thus allowing for miniprograms to air throughout the day. Another springboard for local programming on an ACTS channel are the nationally produced programs on the network from most major Christian denominations. These programs might introduce or complement a local church production.

Along with the positive, Christian programming services, some cable systems offer objectionable programs. This author recently studied listings of satellite-delivered programs available to cable operators. The results were startling: if viewers were to attempt to see every program described as containing "excessive violence, offensive language, nudity" and/or "adult humor," it would take approximately three months of nonstop viewing to see what is available in one month's listings!

Ministers and laypersons have a sizable opportunity. You can become producers of local programming which enhances the family-oriented and religious network sources. These productions will give local citizens a distinct alternative to other less-desirable programs mentioned above.

People *will* watch your local programs when you meet their recognized needs and interests. (Consult the appendix for numerous local origination program ideas.)

Cable Managers Are Interested in Your Program

Why would a local cable manager be open to airing your church's program at little or no cost? Assuming your program is well done and addresses community needs, the manager may be interested for several reasons:

1. Local programming generates interest in cable, resulting in new subscribers. New subscribers mean additional revenue for the company and recognition for the manager.

If your church produces a program featuring local personalities, church members will watch; they will encourage their friends to watch. Local personalities will watch; they will encourage their friends to watch, and so on. This response translates into good news for the cable company.

2. Local managers are usually citizens of your community. They have an interest in the local scene, too. By making your contribution via cable, the community becomes a better place to live for all.

3. Local church programming offers stability in the subscriber base for a cable company. Viewers of religious and local origination programming tend to be faithful and are less likely to discontinue cable subscriptions. "Cable Churn"—the constant turnover in subscriber hookups and

disconnects—is a major concern for cable operators.

4. Cable television is promoted as you encourage people to watch your program. Every time your program is mentioned from the pulpit, in the church mailout, or in the Sunday bulletin, cable gets a free advertisement.

5. Local programming is often difficult to secure, but local governments granting franchises to cable operators want this type of service.

(The Federal Communications Commission required cable operators to have local origination programming for a number of years. Such a requirement is no longer enforced though local governmental bodies still express interest in having this feature.)

6. Cable managers and community leaders are pleased to see money being spent on religious programming which remains in the local economy.

7. Local programming gains goodwill for the cable system. Like any other public utility, cable gets its share of criticism for service outages, equipment problems, billing errors, and so on. When community thought is focused on the benefits brought by cable service, there is a reduction in negative feedback by residents.

What Cable Can Do for Your Church

"Why should our church become involved in cablecasting?" You can surely expect that question at the first mention of the possibility. One of the best answers given is to be found in a leaflet produced by the ACTS Satellite Network, entitled "When ACTS Comes to Town."[8] A paraphrasing of this answer in totally local church terms is shared for your use:

A Continual Presence—As you become involved in cable production, the church is constantly identified within the community. This is a reminder of your presence and purpose.

A Powerful Ally—Cable involvement does not replace any of your existing ministries, but it can strengthen what you do. For instance, if your church has a ministry to homebound individuals, a special Bible study program on cable offers additional opportunity to "enter" the home for another expression of Christian concern. Pastors from churches of several denominations in one Tennessee community rotate responsibility for such a program which is largely targeted to homebound persons.

A Welcomed Image—For churches to get media recognition in some large metropolitan areas almost requires an unfortunate happening like a fire or burglary. Cable involvement, on the other hand, offers a means of cultivating a positive image, especially if the church produces some programs merely for their value to the community. Through production of a local news program (where there is no local television station) or videotaping and replaying of high school football games, for instance, the church proves a genuine interest in the life and progress of the whole community.

An Evangelistic Tool—Cable television will never take the place of a personal visit by someone to share her faith. However, your cable program can be a cultivative tool for planting seeds and expressing concerns for persons.

A Prospect Paradise—Locating prospective members is an ongoing task for churches. By offering an opportunity for individuals to respond to your cablecast, you will discover people searching for a relationship which can be met by a local church family.

A Crisis Center—One of the purposes the church can fulfill is to be a "spiritual and physical first-aid station." If your church has been visible in the community as evidenced by cable involvement, you will be the one who comes to mind when a crisis arises. This recognition of concern opens another door to ministry in a local area.

A Family's Friend—As mentioned earlier, the average household watches fifty hours of television per week. By offering good, family-oriented programming and by supporting network services which provide this type of programming, your church is truly a family's friend.

(One way a church can address this need is through production of a children's program. There is a shortage of good children's programming and a growing need. Children in increasing numbers are being left at home alone while both parents work. Television becomes the "electronic baby-sitter" for the "latchkey" child. How unfortunate! However, what an unparalleled opportunity awaits the church intent on addressing this need!)

A Priceless Platform—Without some external means, the only people who hear the message of the church proclaimed are those present at the regular worship hours. Cable extends to your church a platform of proclamation not available before now.

A Fantastic Investment—What other kind of investment can your church make which yields ongoing access to the homes of your community for a few dollars a week? Even if it becomes necessary to purchase video equipment, the cost is less than sponsoring a series of spot announcements for just one evening on prime-time television in a major metropolitan market. The yield for the one night of spot exposure would be positive. But what about those persons not watching that channel on the particular evening? The same investment in cable would be ongoing with multiplication of exposure possibilities.

(These statements should not be construed as discouraging the use of broadcast or spot announcements. For the church with access and funding, these options will further enhance ministry and outreach.)

A Cooperative Mission—Finally, cable utilization gives church members an opportunity to work together on a mission project of inestimable potential. Additionally, talented members are able to use their creative gifts in the church's ministry. For some, the project may give them the best outlet they have encountered for making a meaningful personal contribution to the church. For others, cable may be a challenge to greater Christian stewardship as they help fund the project.

In even broader terms, cable involvement is a means of area churches working together on a joint mission thrust. By cooperating with one another, the message is still told, and the load is lighter for all.

LPTV—What About It?

Up to this point, discussion of church involvement in television has been limited largely to cable. Possibilities also exist in low-power television (LPTV).

Low power is a relatively new television outlet designed by the Federal Communications Commission to make local television stations available in more locales and to make ownership possible for additional individuals and groups. The coverage area is less for low power (perhaps a twenty-five-mile radius), and so are the start-up costs (possibly much less than two hundred thousand dollars for LPTV vs. well over a million dollars for full-power television). By design, LPTV is a television outlet for local involvement.

If there is a low-power television station in your area, management may welcome your participation as a local programmer. Benefits to the church are similar to cable involvement. Additionally, everyone in the LPTV coverage area who has a television set is able to receive the signal, just as they are able to receive other broadcast channels.

[One caution about LPTV . . . the "low power" of low-power television is exactly what it says. LPTV transmitters operate at a fraction of their "big brothers," full power. Do not expect the quality of signal at considerable distance that you have come to know with other television stations. Hilly terrain and other barriers affect LPTV signals, reducing transmitter range.]

Costs for Cable/LPTV Involvement

At least three variables will influence the financial outlay: cost of air time, cost of equipment, and degree of involvement in cable or LPTV.

Air time may cost little or nothing, depending on cable or LPTV management. Since your church offers the cablecaster/broadcaster numerous benefits (as outlined earlier in the chapter), it is not unreasonable to anticipate a reciprocal attitude by a local manager.

[A suggestion—be positive, flexible, and realistic when approaching local management. Give prior thought to the type of programming you envision, the target audience(s) and how often you actually think you can produce such a program. Numerous opportunities have been lost by inquirers demanding time or making unrealistic requests. Do not expect a manager to totally rearrange his schedule to meet your precise expectations. Unless you have prior television production experience, you are asking the manager to take a risk on an unproven program. On the other hand, this author has found managers to be most interested in locally originated programming, willing to go "above and beyond the call of duty" to help you achieve this objective.]

A second area of possible expense is for equipment. If purchase becomes necessary, you will now find quality video equipment at an affordable price. Actually, equipment costs are continuing to drop while quality is stabilizing or even increasing in some cases. Various denominations have buying groups or time-payment plans to help local churches with selection and purchase. Many video dealers have lease-purchase plans which spread payments over a long period of time and may even allow you to periodically update equipment rather than buying it outright.

[Specific guidelines for purchasing video equipment are given in a later chapter, and various equipment features are outlined in the appendix.]

Another option for securing equipment is rental. If the amount of usage will be limited, rental is a viable choice. Renting equipment gives you an added opportunity to try different models and types before purchase. Scores of equipment owners realize they could have made much wiser purchases if they had known what they know now through experience.

Perhaps the best option is use of the equipment owned by the cable or LPTV operator. In an effort to foster locally originated programs, many cable operators have purchased equipment and even equipped studios which are available to persons wanting to produce local programs. (Some local governments have included such stipulations in their franchising agreements.) So, ask! I have visited with cable managers eager to see their equipment and studios utilized for their intended purposes.

A final financial consideration is for those who have the desire for a broader ministry through cable or LPTV. Churches and groups of churches are discovering that in some cases it may be cost-effective to manage a religious channel or even a low-power television station. With family/religious networks like the ACTS Satellite Network making available blocks of time for local origination programming, churches are finding it possible to offer quality local and national programming. By selling spot announcements to recover the cost of operations, this becomes a feasible plan.

Churches of all sizes successfully manage local origination channels from within their church buildings. For example, a small United Methodist church in Mississippi operates a channel which has gained such widespread viewership that local parades are rerouted by the church to receive live cable television coverage. The entire operation is staffed by volunteers.

Cablecasting and LPTV broadcasting are an entire new avenue to ministry for anyone willing to commit time and energy. Is it possible your church could become involved or enlarge its involvement with this means of communicating the gospel?

Notes

1. "Cable Industry Growth Chart," *CableVision*, 26 Nov. 1984, p. 86. Source: CableProFile Data Base, International Communications Research.
2. "Cable Industry Growth Chart," *CableVision*, 26 Nov. 1984, p. 86. Source: CableProFile Data Base, International Communications Research.
3. Joan Hanauer, "Network's Share of TV Audience Drops," *Alexandria-Daily Town Talk*, 8 Dec. 1984, p. 21.
4. "BBDO Predicts Network Shares will Drop to 65%," *Broadcasting*, 12 Dec. 1983, p. 35.
5. Louis Chunovic, "The Decline of Network Dominance," *CableVision*, 3 Dec. 1984, p. 31. Source: A. C. NIELSON for CAD.
6. Louis Chunovic, "The Decline of Network Dominance," *CableVision*, 3 Dec. 1984, p. 36.
7. *Broadcasting Yearbook*, 1984.
8. "When ACTS Comes to Town," Broadcast Services Department, ACTS Satellite Network, Fort Worth, Texas.

4
Selecting Video Equipment for Religious Education and Church Programming

One of the most frustrating aspects of becoming involved in video can be the purchase of equipment. It always seems someone has just introduced a "revolutionary new design" or "far superior product." If you buy today, a competitor offers a similar or better product tomorrow for less money.

I frequently receive telephone calls and am asked in conferences about purchasing video equipment. Here are some of the questions: "With prices coming down and new features being added, should we wait to purchase new equipment?" "What brands should we buy?" "How can we be assured of having 'state-of-the-art' equipment?" "What is the best price?" This chapter is designed to answer these and other equipment-related questions. Beyond this, there is information shared about common features on types of video equipment. Understanding available features will help you make comparisons among the various models and to select the unit which meets your needs at the best price.

"Should We Wait?" Waiting for the video market to stabilize is futile. A backlog of new video ideas and designs has existed for years. Since the public can only absorb so much at once, manufacturers regularly dole out new features. Hesitating to purchase in expectation of new features is merely depriving the church of enjoying benefits from video in religious education, church programming, and outreach.

Regarding price decreases, probably no greater price break will exist in educational video recording equipment than now. With expiration of VHS licensing agreements, 1985 brought a flood of low-priced units from overseas sources such as Korea and Taiwan. Japanese manufacturers, long the source of most video equipment used in this country, have turned their attention toward broadening the array of new features, increasing audio and video quality, and creating smaller, lighter units. Costs for these technological advances will likely stabilize price declines.

"What Brand?" Americans have long been admonished to buy name brands. There is wisdom in this axiom for video purchasers. Choose products from a company with a reputation for honoring its warranty. A greater question, however, is: "Who manufactured the product?" Some people are surprised to learn most video recorders are manufactured in Japan by just a few companies. It is not unusual for several brand names to be coming out of the same manufacturing facility. Additionally, some major brand name VCR's are not necessarily manufactured by the same company each year. The contract may be awarded to another manufacturer periodically.

"State of the Art?" Churches cannot always have "state-of-the-art" equipment. A check with major television networks reveals even they do not have "state-of-the-art" equipment in every case. A far greater concern for churches is that the video meets current needs and is expandable to meet future needs as envisioned by church leadership.

There will always be some new, exciting features (or "bells and whistles" as they are called in the video industry). What should be more exciting is securing quality products which satisfy your requirements. Wise purchases make it possible to grow into a larger system as the ministry expands.

"State of the art" may ultimately be more of a "state of mind" than a necessity. Quality equipment at a good price is the goal, *and* it is good stewardship, too!

"Best Price?" Price is based largely on quality, number of features, and, to some degree, competition. When you familiarize yourself with capabilities and compare them with your needs, it becomes simpler to determine the "best price." Buying the least expensive video recorder, for example, *may* prove to be a mistake *if* needed features are not included on the selected unit. Conversely, buying the most expensive unit *may not* be the best expenditure of funds *if* many unnecessary features are included on the unit.

The Foremost Question—Although all of the previous questions are important in the selection process, the first question ought to be: "What do I want to do with the equipment?" A satisfactory answer to this query influences all other decisions.

The remainder of this chapter is designed to give you benchmarks for making educational video equipment selections. Because of the diversity of applications, another entire chapter is dedicated to selecting equipment for cablecasting/broadcasting. More details on equipment features are given in this educational video chapter section since cablecasting/broadcasting applications vary widely. Decisions for securing cablecasting/broadcasting equipment may also be influenced by availability of and compatibility with existing equipment at the cable company or low-power television station.

The Selection Process

Separating educational and cablecasting/broadcasting applications of video is difficult since some equipment may serve dual roles. However, this approach seems more useful for those contemplating only educational video or cablecasting/broadcasting.

The following are some of the major components which may be included in the church's use of video in education:[1]

Videocassette Recorder

As with selection of all other video equipment, the first question relates to intended use. Your choice of recorder is particularly important. Such equipment will enable you to accomplish the chosen task or severely limit this accomplishment. Will you be playing prerecorded tapes? A video player (not recorder) can serve this purpose. (Many video players are now available at far less cost than recorders.)

Will you be recording from broadcast or cablecast television? A tuner/timer would be desirable to allow for unattended recording from cable, broadcast television, or satellite. (See appendix for guidance on use of copyrighted material.)

Will you be duplicating noncopyrighted tapes? If so, you will need a source machine and a videocassette recorder. Both machines will not have to have all of the "bells and whistles." The source machine could be a player only.

Will you be recording from a satellite-delivered service? Will you be producing in-house training tapes which require use of an editor? Does the machine need to be *portable* (battery operated and more costly), simply *movable* (transportable but not requiring electricity), or a *fixed unit* (not easily moved and requiring electricity)?

Consideration will not be given to the one-inch (reel-to-reel) recorder or its decreasingly popular older brother, two-inch. Their usage for local church education would be "overkill." Possible videocassette formats to consider are:

U-matic (three-quarter-inch)—This format is the most broadly used for making master tapes for educational video. Since its introduction in the 1970s, U-matic has revolutionized educational video and is dually used in cablecast/broadcast applications. If you are going to be doing a large amount of educational taping, editing, and dubbing (duplicating), a three-quarter-inch recorder is desirable. If not, the cost of three-quarter-inch equipment may be prohibitive (more than twice that of half-inch equipment). Since half-inch editors are now available (also at less cost than three-quarter-inch), most churches not considering cablecasting or widespread duplication and distribution may wish to invest in half-inch equipment. For those purchasing three-quarter inch, ask yourself about the need for these features:

1. *Portable* [battery operated]

Illustration 11

Example of a portable VHS video player (courtesy of PortaVideo International, Inc., Phoenix, Arizona).

Illustration 12

Common connectors used in video (left to right): male mini phone (audio plug), RCA-type male and female (consumer equipment), F-type male and female (consumer and industrial), BNC male and female (industrial), and UHF male and female (industrial).
300 OHM to 75 OHM Transformer (left corner), used to connect many videocassette recorders to television sets.
Signal Splitter (right corner), used for joining two television sets to one videocassette recorder; two television sets to one antenna; etc.

2. *Random access* [ability to find a particular place on a videotape electronically without viewing it]
3. *Playback only* [for viewing-only situations. Such a unit has no recording function.] (See illustration 11.)
4. *Edit Capabilities* [Can it be used with an edit controller? If so, will it serve as the more expensive full-edit machine or the less-expensive source machine? If neither of these, will it backspace edit? (See glossary.)]
5. *Picture search* [ability to see picture during playback at faster speed]
6. *Loading type* [Does the videocassette load into the machine from the top or front? If the machine is to be stored on a rack or shelf with other pieces of equipment, front loading is preferable since it takes less space and the tape is more accessible.]
7. *Time base corrector jack* [Does the recorder have a place to directly connect a time base corrector (TBC)? A TBC corrects variances in signal among pieces of input equipment such as cameras and recorders. (A full explanation of TBC's may be found later in the text.)]
8. *Audio dub jack* [does the recorder have a connection for inputting an audio source such as a microphone or audiotape player for dubbing audio onto a tape? This will allow you to later add new sound or additional sound without erasing the picture.]
9. *RF modulator* [This device turns video signals into regular channel frequencies usable on a standard television set. Without an RF modulator, you must use a more expensive monitor for viewing tapes since a television set cannot use "raw" video signals (see glossary).]
10. *Connector types* [Does the machine have consumer or industrial/professional connectors? Professional connectors such as eight-pin, BNC, F-type, and even the less-used UHF are more desirable for linking to other professional equipment such as monitors. Adapters are available for mismatches. Consumer connectors are usually RCA type. Sometimes, miniphone connectors are used for audio input on consumer machines (see illustration 12 and also glossary regarding connectors).]
11. *Counter* [Is the tape-counting device of a mechanical type with wheels that turn by a system of gears or an electronic/LED type which simply projects numbers on a screen? Does the counter have a time-elapsed feature to indicate how much time is left before the tape runs out?]
12. *Drive mechanism*—[Are moving parts driven by the older belt method, a direct drive, or a servo which permits instant attainment of speed for use in editing?]
13. *Audio gain limiting*—[Does the machine automatically limit extremes of audio gain (sound), or does it have the superior method which combines automatic audio gain limiting with switchable to manual control for special applications?]
14. *Remote control*—[Does the unit have the capability of being operated with a remote control? If so, how many functions are operated by the remote control?]
15. *Automatic inserter capable*—[Will the unit accept a computer-controlled automatic inserter? These inserters are mostly used for placing spots or programs onto cable channels without operator assistance. Inserters may have some applications for satellite-delivered educational services, too. Caution: most machines do not have this feature, and inserters are designed to work with certain recorder models. Unless you plan to use an inserter, this feature is not important.]
16. *Tuner/timer*—[Can the recorder receive television signals with an internal tuner and automatically record programs at specified times? This feature is helpful for recording satellite-delivered or broadcast educational programs without an operator. Most three-quarter-inch recorder models no longer have tuner/timers.]

VHS (half-inch)—The VHS recorder is one of

two half-inch formats, the other being Beta or Betamax. Though Beta was the first half-inch videocassette recorder, the majority of half-inch recorders now being used educationally and in homes are VHS. Several producers of religious education video materials have selected VHS as their distribution format. One example is the Southern Baptist Video Tape Service.

VHS and Beta videotapes are the same width, but the two cassettes are *not interchangeable*. VHS and Beta both have three speeds for recording and playback though VHS has the greater playing time with its longest tape. Prices for both half-inch formats are similar.

[A word of caution: modified high-speed versions of both VHS and Beta have been produced for cablecasters and broadcasters. Combination camera/recorders are available for such broadcast applications, but the tapes produced are not compatible with educational/consumer playback units. There are now, however, camera/recorder combinations available for educational and consumer applications which play at standard speed and are compatible with other equipment. Also, some camera/recorder combinations feature a VHS-C cassette which is much smaller, thus allowing for a smaller recorder. This VHS-C cassette will fit a regular VHS recorder when equipped with an adapter.] (See illustration 13.)

For sake of space, evaluation criteria will only be given for VHS half-inch equipment. However the same basic considerations apply to Beta.

Three major determinants of price for a VHS recorder are: (1) *the number and type of video heads on the unit,* (2) *the capabilities of the tuner/timer,* and (3) *the capabilities of the remote control.*

Video heads are the heart of a videocassette recorder. They are the electromagnetic devices responsible for recording the picture and playing it back. The playback head(s) may be called upon to reproduce the picture at regular speed, faster than normal, slower than normal, or to freeze-frame for detailed study. [Some units now have capabilities for playing back a picture at multiple high and slow speeds.]

If a recorder has only two heads, all of the special functions must be performed by the same playback head. This leads to significant head wear when the numerous special functions are used regularly. Should you plan to merely play tapes without exercising special options, a two-head machine may be fine. However, recorders with more heads are able to assign special functions to each one, thus reducing head wear. Since replacement of heads can cost almost half as much as some recorders, be certain to care for them.

Churches planning to use their recorders frequently ought to consider purchasing an industrial unit. The cost is not much greater, but the heads are heavier duty. [A word of caution—many industrial units only play at the fastest or "professional" speed, thus yielding the best picture. Tapes from professional video libraries will be recorded at this speed. Tapes from other sources, however, may be recorded at one of the other speeds and will not replay properly on a single-speed unit. Check speed capabilities before purchasing a recorder.]

Tuner/timers are a second price determinant of VHS recorders. Most tuners enable the VCR to receive regular and cable channels, hence they are called "cable ready." Be certain to purchase a VCR with "cable ready" capability.

Some recorders are only able to receive twelve preselected channels. To watch a different channel, one of the existing channel slots must be reallocated to the new channel. (This is usually not a problem. Viewers will often have a few favorite channels which they watch regularly. However, with cable television offering thirty or more channels, the process of retuning can be cumbersome.)

Other recorders have a capability of tuning in any channel by simply pressing the appropriate numbers into the VCR control panel or remote control unit.

The "timer" of "tuner/timer" refers to the ability of a recorder to record programs without the presence of an operator. These timers are rated by the number of events. Each occasion when the recorder comes on, records the program, and goes off is called *one event*. If the recorder has a one-event/seven-day timer, this means the recorder can turn itself on at a time predetermined by the operator,

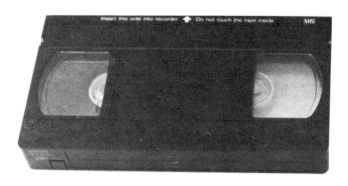  

Illustration 13

Size comparisons (left to right): ½″ VHS videocassette, ½″ VHS-C videocassette, and standard audiocassette. (photo by R. Chip Turner)

Illustration 14

Four of the current videocassette formats are (left to right): 8 mm, ½″ VHS, ½″ Beta, and ¾″ U-matic.

record a program, and go off in the course of a seven-day span. (Some one-event units also have the capability of coming on at the same time every day within the stated time without resetting the timer.)

If you contemplate the need to record more than one event and/or you need a longer time span to be covered, units are available—at a greater price, of course. [One note: most users are not likely in need of a unit which will come on a large number of times within a several-week span. You will run out of tape on the VCR before you exhaust the event/day limit. A three- or four-event timer is probably adequate for most applications.)

Remote control capabilities are a third key-price determinant of VHS units. A basic remote control will merely place the recorder in the pause mode. At the other end of the spectrum is a remote control which will perform every function available on the machine itself. Wireless remote control recorders are obviously more expensive than the wired models.

With the three key-price determinants in mind, use the following list of VHS features as a checklist to determine the unit which meets your need:

1. *Number of heads* [see text above]
2. *Tuner type* [A few recorders are still available with click-type tuners similar to television sets. The electronic tuners (push button) are preferable since they have no moving parts to wear out or corrode.]
3. *Tuner location* [On some portable recorders, tuners are a separate, add-on piece rather than an integral part of the unit. Such a design reduces the weight of the piece which must be carried around. If for some reason you envision always needing a tuner with the recorder "in the field" and are willing to carry additional weight, a few portable VCRs have internal tuners.]
4. *Tuner availability* [Is the tuner included in the price of the portable unit, or is it an option? Units other than portable usually include the tuner as a standard feature.]
5. *Tuner capabilities* [Are there certain channels preset into the recorder which require adjustment to receive another channel, or can any channel be received by simply "punching in" the channel number? Will the recorder receive all cable channels (without a converter box) as well as regular channels? (There are a few cable companies which use another type of cable frequency, but they are rare. In such a case, a converter box is needed, so ask your cable operator.)]
6. *Timer capabilities*—[How many events over how many days will the timer operate the recorder?]
7. *Mobility of unit* [Is the unit truly portable, simply movable or fixed?]
8. *Picture search* [This is one of many names for a feature which allows a viewer to watch the picture in a faster speed—forward or reverse—while "searching" for a certain spot on the tape. Some recorders have a search feature without picture which is much less desirable and more time consuming for operators. Most units have picture search at little or no extra cost, so do not settle for less!]
9. *Remote control* [See text above.]
10. *Audio* [Improved audio has finally come to video recorders. There are several choices in three categories: (1) monaural, (2) stereo, and (3) Dolby. Another feature which proves useful for some educational applications is two audio channels. This allows a second channel to be used for an additional language, music, more commentary, or operation instructions.]
11. *Audio dub* [This capability allows the operator to add or change audio on a videotape after it has been shot by a camera or recorded from another video source. Audio dub is especially useful for adding the desired sound in a more controlled environment than the one in which the program was taped earlier.]
12. *Loading type* [Is the videotape loaded into the recorder from the top or front? Front loading is useful when there is limited space above the recorder.]
13. *Counter* [See the discussion under number

11 of three-quarter-inch recorders for an explanation of mechanical and electronic counters and the "time-elapsed" feature. Additionally, many VHS counters have a memory function. "Memory" enables the operator to set the counter on zero and to return to this point at any time by pressing "rewind" or "fast forward." The recorder will automatically stop at zero.

14. *Connectors* [Are the connectors of professional type—BNC, UHF, eight-pin, and F-type—or consumer: RCA and miniphone? Consumer-type connectors will link more easily with a regular television. Adapters are available, however. (See glossary for explanations of various connectors.)]

15. *Edit capabilities* [Will the recorder function with an editor? If so, does the VCR have the capability of being the more expensive full-edit or the less expensive source machine? Virtually all recorders will do a backspace edit which eliminates picture breakup by backing up momentarily before recording. This movement backward allows the recorder to erase the last few seconds of the previously recorded material and link the two scenes together without a loss of picture stability.]

16. *Random access* [Does the recorder have the necessary circuitry to "find" a predetermined place on a tape by receiving instructions from the operator? Can the recorder be linked to a personal computer for interactive video?]

17. *Speeds* [Does the recorder have all three VHS speeds for recording and playback—*slowest* for tape economy and length of recording time, *intermediate* for speed and quality compromise, and *fastest* for highest quality picture—or merely the fastest speed (which is considered "professional" speed)? On *some* recorders, these speeds are called SP (standard play), LP (long play), and SLP (super long play). Caution: tapes secured from tape libraries will generally be recorded at the SP speed since the best picture quality is delivered at this high speed. However, if you will be using tape sources other than professional libraries, you may not want to purchase a single-speed VCR.]

18. *Rewind* [Does the recorder automatically rewind when it reaches the end of the tape? Some recorders will also rewind to a predetermined setting. An additional feature on still others allows for continuous play and rewind (excellent for displays).]

19. *Camera ready* [Virtually all VHS recorders will accept a camera. Since most cameras operate on DC current, however, an expensive adapter is required if the recorder does not provide such a DC outlet for the camera. Generally, VCRs require an adapter unless they are portable units which have DC capability.]

20. *Service* [Is service by factory-trained personnel available locally? If not, how about within your area? Long delays, necessitated by shipping equipment for servicing, are frustrating to regular users. Shipping is not advised for delicate equipment either.]

21. *Basic design* [Ultimately, you need to find equipment which is easy to operate by others as well as yourself. If not, you will increase the need for service which is precipitated by misuse. And, find out from others how reliably the model you like has performed in the field. Experience has proven it unwise to purchase new, untried models or models with a poor performance record.]

Other Format Recorders—Numerous other recorders are on the market besides VHS and Beta. Since the majority of educators are seeking to standardize distribution by choosing VHS (or in a few cases VHS and Beta), little space is given to other formats. This is not meant to downgrade quality or capabilities. For those wishing to make comparisons, the VHS checklist is a good measuring device. A few of the other formats are:

1. *Video 2000*—is the European response to VHS and Beta. Though Video 2000 cas-

settes use half-inch tape, they are not interchangeable with VHS or Beta.
2. *Quarter Inch*—may be useful for very compact applications but is not much smaller than VHS or Beta. [Since VHS has come out with a VHS-C cassette which is even smaller than VHS, size is not much of a redeeming factor for one-quarter inch. VHS-C cassettes will play on regular VHS equipment with an adapter. Their small size allows the C-type recorder to be quite small.]
3. *Eight Millimeter*—is largely for home video use. (See illustration 14.) Eight millimeter does not jeopardize VHS as the leader in educational applications. Though not originally touted as an educational format by the manufacturers of eight millimeter, some use will undoubtedly be made of it in this manner.

Monitor, Receiver, or Large Screen

The only other necessary piece of equipment for using prerecorded videotapes is a picture reproduction device. Before selecting a television set, monitor, or projection television system, ask yourself the basic question: "What do I want to do with it?" Included in your answer is where you plan to use the equipment. Overall, a television set offers the most flexibility for the price.

Quality and price of projection television systems have improved to the point of making them attractive. If funds are available, several excellent buys are now in the marketplace.

Should funding be limited, remember that as you acquaint others with the values of video as an educational tool you will have need for several additional video units (recorder, television, and rolling cart). For the price of one video projection system, you can buy several additional video-viewing units, especially if you purchase video players instead of full recorders. [Video players are now readily available at reasonable prices.] For larger group viewing, a number of television sets can be joined together with a signal (RF) splitter and coaxial cable. Consider these features when selecting television sets or monitors:
1. *Monitor or receiver* [Feeling is divided on whether users of educational video should use monitors or receivers. Monitors receive "raw" video signals from a camera or recorder with excellent reproduction of picture. They may also feature special inputs for additional audio sources and microphones. Output jacks for audio and video make it easy to add other machines, amplification systems, and so on. "Professional" connectors easily link with other industrial equipment. However, if you are using a consumer-type VCR which does not provide "audio out" jacks, you have a problem! Monitors will not accept RF modulated signals (regular TV channel 3 or 4) which are provided by the recorder. And consumer recorders do not accept eight-pin or BNC connectors. Therefore, a television set may be your safest option.]

Receivers—regular television sets—are less costly than monitors. They produce an acceptable picture. And consumer VCRs are actually designed to be used with regular television sets. Televisions can even be used as viewers for recording with a camera because of improved circuitry in videocassette recorders. Moreover, a television set is available for other purposes when not connected to the recorder while a monitor is virtually useless in such a circumstance.

[Actually, the best possible combination is a monitor/receiver which gives you all of the flexibility of the monitor and all of the consumer conveniences of a television set, but cost becomes a factor.]
2. *Color or monochrome* [There is no doubt that using a monochrome (black-and-white) television set reduces effectiveness of a presentation. This is a color-oriented age. Video productions intentionally feature shades of color to impart subtle messages. And producers rarely give thought to what a program will look like in black and white. As obvious as this may seem, the author periodically finds monochrome television sets in use in educational settings though the cost of color equipment is little more.
3. *Cabinet* [Is the cabinet made of metal or

plastic? Metal cabinetry is preferable for durability. If the receiver is securely mounted (bolted on) to a rolling cart, the cabinet composition is not as crucial since it will be protected from abuse.]
4. *Power source* [If the receiver is to be used for monitoring a recording with a portable VCR in the field, it must be adaptable to use DC current.]
5. *Picture size* [Churches are encouraged to buy receivers with as large a screen as possible to make them adaptable to most viewing situations. Twenty-five-inch sets are widely available and adaptable to use on rolling carts. The receivers which use a flat screen rather than a picture tube may be a viable option, too.]
6. *Speakers* [Choose receivers with multiple speakers which project toward the audience. Intensity and quality of sound are impacted by small speakers which project through the sides. You may want a stereo unit, too.]

When considering purchase of a video projection system, these are some of the features:
1. *Mounting* [Until the mid-1980s, most video projectors were stationary, either in a cabinet on the floor with a self-contained screen or mounted from the ceiling. Both the ceiling-mounted variety and the floor model with front or rear projection are still quite serviceable if the projection unit is intended to remain in one area. Video projectors are now available, however, which are truly portable. Weighing about the same and costing little more than a 16mm movie projector, these units have a self-contained video playback system and project an image on a screen or wall. (If there is a self-contained playback unit in the projector, be sure to check the format before purchase.) Single-tube units eliminate most adjustments which plague some three-tube units.]
2. *Resolution/brightness* [The "bottom lines" are: (1) How clearly defined is the picture, and (2) Is it bright enough for all to see? Early video projection systems were limited on both counts—clarity and brightness. Ask to have the projection system demonstrated in your facility before purchase.]
3. *Switchable image* [Does the unit have a switch which reverses the image for a rear screen projection? Such a feature is required if you ever use rear screen. Sometimes light is easier to contain in a rear screen setup. If the projector's image is not reversible, everything will be backward when projected from behind the screen.
4. *Projection distance/size* [How far will the system project a usable picture, and what size picture do you get at this distance? Is it large enough to deliver an image which is no less than one sixth as wide as the distance to the rear of the room (optimum viewing size)? The ratio should be no less than one to six (1:6).]
5. *Screen type* [Is a special screen required, or can you use existing projection screens or even a light-colored wall?]
6. *Speakers* [How many speakers are in the system? Do they deliver adequate sound for the size of audience which the picture serves, and are the speakers directed toward the audience?]
7. *Remote control* [Does the system have a remote control? Is it wired or wireless? Does it control all functions or only selected ones?]

Video Cameras

Choosing a video camera is a very important step requiring a sense of direction for now and the foreseeable future. As an example, if you envision using two or more cameras together, this will influence camera choice. Also, you will choose entirely different cameras if they are to be used for cablecasting/broadcasting, too. Since the intent of this chapter is to address entry-level equipment for educational video, however, the assumption is made that one camera is to be used to "feed" one video recorder. Moreover, the price range will be from a few hundred dollars to less than three thousand dollars. Consider these features:
1. *Color or monochrome* [As in television receivers, do not buy black-and-white equipment in

this color world! There is really little cost difference.]

2. *Viewfinder* [The most common viewfinders are optical and electronic. An *optical viewfinder* is usually a hole in the camera body which has been positioned so that the operator sees approximately what the "camera lens" sees. This is a less accurate viewfinder system. The cameraman has no indication of what the pickup tube is sensing of the subject.

An *electronic viewfinder* is a small picture tube which indicates exactly what the camera is "seeing" except that the picture is in black and white. If there is too little lighting, contrast, etc., this is obvious to the operator. An added bonus on most cameras equipped with electronic viewfinders is that they may serve as a small monitor to view the tape after shooting a scene.]

3. *Pickup tubes/CCD* [The pickup tubes are the heart of a camera. Because of the cost of three-tube cameras, beginner-level educational producers have leaned toward one-tube models. In three-tube cameras, one tube is dedicated to each of the primary colors (red, green, and blue). A one-tube camera requires a single tube to handle the entire work load.]

[Three developments are now influencing camera purchases with regard to tubes or charged coupled devices (CCD's): *(1) high quality single-tube cameras are delivering satisfactory performance levels at a reasonable rate. (2) Tubes in three-tube cameras are decreasing in size and price, making less expensive three-tube cameras available for local churches able to pay approximately $3,000 per camera. (3) A new camera technology using CCD's—charged coupled devices—is now available* (see glossary). These CCD's are used in place of pickup tubes. As technology grows, this may be a viable alternative for price and physical size reductions. (One word of caution: it may be possible for a camera to be too small. An ultrasmall, light camera is difficult to hold and move steadily. Try several models and sizes before purchasing one.)]

If you are just entering educational video production, a single-tube camera costing less than $1,000 will likely meet your needs. You will be able to gain valuable, firsthand experience while producing attractive tapes. As you expand involvement in the future, the camera will still be valuable for certain applications.

4. *Lines of resolution* [This measurement indicates the amount of detail or clarity you may expect in a television picture. Cameras producing more lines of resolution than others are "feeding" a recorder additional picture signal information. Know how many lines of resolution your recorder can process, too. If the camera can give significantly more lines of resolution than your recorder can accept, this is "overkill."]

5. *Light sensitivity* [Most video cameras are now touted as "low light" models. You can compare models by asking how many "footcandles," "lux," or "lumens" of light (see glossary) are required to produce a satisfactory picture. The lower the number, the greater the ability to operate in low-light situations. A better test for low-light capability is to compare picture quality of cameras focused on the same object at the same light level. Check not only for brightness but also for clarity. Is the picture too "grainy" or poorly defined for your purposes? (One note: some situations require that you not add light to the setting. Yet you can virtually always add clarity and color to an indoor taping with supplemental lighting.) Use lights designed for video so colors do not become distorted in the taping.]

6. *Iris control* [The "iris" controls the amount of light entering the lens. Most cameras have an automatic iris which adjusts the aperture (the size of opening for light to enter the lens) each time the light level changes. Insist on a camera with a manual override so you can adjust for unusual lighting circumstances or for special effects.]

7. *Signal-to-noise ratio* [This is a comparison between the level of the recorded video signal and the noise level in the picture caused by the recording process. Picture

"noise" will be seen as static or snow. A quality camera produces a low noise level and a high picture level, hence a better picture.]

8. *Lens* [Having a good lens on your camera can make up for some other inadequacies. Insist on a zoom lens, *not* a fixed-focus lens. Make sure the ratio of magnification is at least six-to-one (6:1) or preferably eight-to-one (8:1). This ratio of magnification will give you more flexibility and require less movement of the camera from location to location. A motorized zoom is superior to a manual zoom when trying to attain smooth movement. If you choose an automatic focus camera, insist that it have a manual override switch. Certain settings, backgrounds, and lighting conditions "trick" an automatic focusing mechanism. You will want to be able to focus manually in these situations.]

9. *Connectors* [Your camera will come with a plug which fits certain recorders. Be careful to see that: (1) your camera will plug into the recorder before purchase and (2) the camera and recorder function properly together. Some cameras have plugs which fit recorders but the camera and recorder do not function properly together. For instance, plugging certain brands of cameras into other recorders makes indicator lights operate in reverse. When the light in your viewfinder indicates the VCR is functioning, it is actually stopped, and vice versa.]

[If the camera plug does not fit the recorder, adapters are available, some costing several hundred dollars.]

10. *White balance method* [A video camera is able to determine proper color balance when it is "told" two things: (1) what type of light is being used (fluorescent, regular incandescent, quartz, and so forth) and (2) what white "looks like." Once a camera is "shown" something white, it "knows" how to balance all other colors. Some cameras are white balanced by pointing the camera toward a white object and holding a button until an indicator light comes on. Other cameras constantly balance white. The user will want a camera which easily and accurately achieves white balance.]

11. *Character generator* [Many consumer-type cameras feature an internal character generator. This device enables you to place titles on your video pictures. A choice of character colors is often available. Check the methods of selecting characters, too. On some models is a button for each letter of the alphabet, the numbers, and a few punctuation marks. Other cameras require you to laboriously press one or two buttons to run through the entire alphabet before coming to the correct letter.]

12. *Tripod and head* [Choosing a tripod and tripod head are an important part of achieving satisfaction with a camera. Get a sturdy tripod, preferably one which has a dolly (rolling) base or capability for adding one. (The larger the tires on the dolly, the smoother will be the roll. This is an important consideration when taping while the camera is in motion.) If you can afford a fluid head rather than a friction head for your tripod, the camera's vertical and horizontal movement will be smoother (see glossary). Saving a few dollars on a less-expensive tripod and tripod head will be a short-term solution and a long-term headache.]

Videodisc Players

Videodisc players offer another facet of video usage to the church leader. Though there are few videodiscs yet available for use in religious education, there is enormous potential. As the cost of producing a videodisc has steadily decreased, opportunity for church leaders to employ this new technology has risen proportionately.

(Though several types of videodiscs have been introduced with some already disappearing from the market, descriptions of videodisc capabilities and functions in this discussion will be limited to the LaserVision (LV) format. The LV videodisc has been chosen for use by most educators because of its superior capabilities. As other formats improve, they may bear further investigation.

One exciting facet of the videodisc is its storage capacity—over one hundred thousand frames or pages on a two-sided disc about the size of a standard record album. Imagine how many books could be stored on one disc! For example, the Library of Congress is aggressively using videodiscs to alleviate their storage problems.

A second promising attribute for videodisc is its ability to interact with the user. Since every frame on the disc is assigned a number, the videodisc player can instantaneously find its specific reference point. In conjunction with a personal computer, the videodisc player guides learners through a session at their own pace and skill levels. A computer directs progress in a learning activity based on the user's response.

A third "plus" of videodisc is its durability. A LaserVision videodisc player operates by means of a laser beam which "reads" reflective patterns of light from indentions or pits on the disc's surface. Since nothing ever touches the disc, its life span is virtually endless. (One of the disadvantages of other types of videodisc players is that a stylus actually "reads" a disc in a manner similar to phonograph records. This stylus or needle riding in the disc's grooves causes wear.)

A fourth benefit of videodisc players is the excellent maintenance record as compared with videocassette recorders.

The only obvious disadvantage of videodisc is that it is a playback unit only. Usage of videodiscs has been limited to prerecorded material. Progress is being made on videodisc recorders. When such units will be available at an affordable price is yet to be known, however.

As you shop for videodisc players, look for these key features:
1. *Format* [LV has been the format for educational applications with interactive capabilities. If you consider another disc format, compare capabilities with the text above.]
2. *Random access* [You definitely want the unit to be capable of instantly accessing all the information on one side of a disc.]
3. *Interactive* [Choose a unit which is able to interact with a popular brand of personal computer with applicable software.]
4. *Sound* [Some units have stereo sound. This feature offers other flexibility afforded by the two audio tracks.]
5. *Frame/title display* [Choose a unit which displays the frame number and title, an important feature for research and interactive functions.]

Computers

This book is not primarily concerned with computer usage except as it relates to interactive educational applications. Yet computers *do* employ video technology even in the display of data on a video screen.

Personal computers are the type under consideration. These small, inexpensive tools are being used for a variety of church religious education tasks. (See the appendix for a sampling of programs now available for the personal computer.)

Briefly described, here are a few features to consider:
1. *Software availability* [Many experienced computer users say that software availability is ultimately more important than computer brand. Begin by using the source directory in the appendix of this book and talking with computer enthusiasts. If you cannot find the type of software desired, do not purchase hardware under the assumption that the software is available "somewhere."]
2. *Interactive* [Be certain the hardware will interact with video recorders and/or videodisc players. Check with computer dealers and suppliers beforehand.]
3. *Data storage* [Does the computer have the capability of using floppy disks as well as cassettes? Disks operate much faster than cassettes.]
4. *Memory capability* [Choose a computer with at least 64 K (kilobytes). Interactive video may take a significant portion of the memory capacity. How much ROM (read only memory) and RAM (random access memory) are available on the chosen model? (See glossary.) Does the memory on this computer meet or exceed the needs of available software?
5. *Monitor* [Is the monitor built in? If so, you

can expect the computer to cost more than one which requires an external monitor. Also, can you use a regular television set you may already have available? Most personal computers do deliver an RF signal for such purposes.]
6. *Peripherals* [When pricing computers, include the needed peripherals in estimating cost. Some of the peripherals are: monitor (if not built-in), disk drive, data cassette player, printer, light pen, and drawing pad (see glossary).]
7. *Printer* [You will want a printer of some type. The two most popular are *daisy wheel* and *dot matrix* (see glossary). Keep in mind that a daisy wheel printer may deliver a crisper copy than some dot matrix printers, but it will not reproduce graphics. Also, most dot matrix printers are faster than daisy wheel printers.]
8. *Training/service* [Equally important to availability of software are local access to training and computer service. You can become frustrated if knowledgeable personnel are not nearby to answer questions and to offer formal training courses. And, as skill increases, you will become dependent on the computer system. Local, rapid service is essential for you.]

TVROs (Satellite "Dishes")

If your church is not already involved in satellite usage, you will probably find yourself using this technology. Several of your members may already have satellite dishes. With the wealth of religious education and other church programming on satellite, the finest teachers are available to churches of every size and every locale. The initial equipment investment is relatively small and upkeep is minimal. Here are some features to consider in comparison shopping:
1. *Signal-to-noise ratio* [In the process of sending a signal of only a few watts in strength to a satellite 22,500 miles over the equator, receiving it back within a split second and amplifying it to a usable level, there is much potential for gaining interference or "noise." One performance comparison which can be made is the signal-to-noise ratio. How much signal are you getting with how much noise? The lower the noise (or interference) level, the better the system.]
2. *Wind load rating* [The satellite dish (or "parabolic antenna") should be able to withstand winds well in excess of one hundred miles per hour and to deliver a quality picture in sustained winds of approximately forty miles per hour.
3. *Composition of dish (or antenna)* [Dishes are now made of wire mesh, fiberglass-coated metallic cloth, solid aluminum, or even metal on a wooden frame. Opinion varies widely on the best type. Weather conditions in your area may influence this decision. For instance, will ice form in the dish and destroy its curvature? Or, will a constant wind load cause the dish to vibrate significantly?]

Your greater concern is the efficiency of the dish's curvature. In other words, as the signal from the satellite reaches your dish, strikes the surface, bounces, and is focused to the feedhorn mounted in front of the dish, how much of the signal is actually received by the system? The larger and more perfectly shaped the dish, the greater the efficiency.
4. *Size of dish* [More satellite signals for church use will likely come from regular communications satellites than from the few high-powered direct broadcast satellites designed for sending programs directly to homes by means of small dishes. One source of satellite-delivered religious education and other church programming, Baptist Telecommunication Network (BTN), suggests a minimum of a ten-foot (or three-meter) dish for the continental United States. A larger dish may be needed in south Texas and south Florida. Alaska and Hawaii definitely require larger equipment.]
5. *Low noise amplifier (LNA)* [The low noise amplifier receives the weak satellite signal from the feedhorn. (See illustration 15.) The feedhorn is the signal-gathering device mounted in front of the dish at the focal point (area expected to receive the greatest intensity of signal bounced off the dish).]

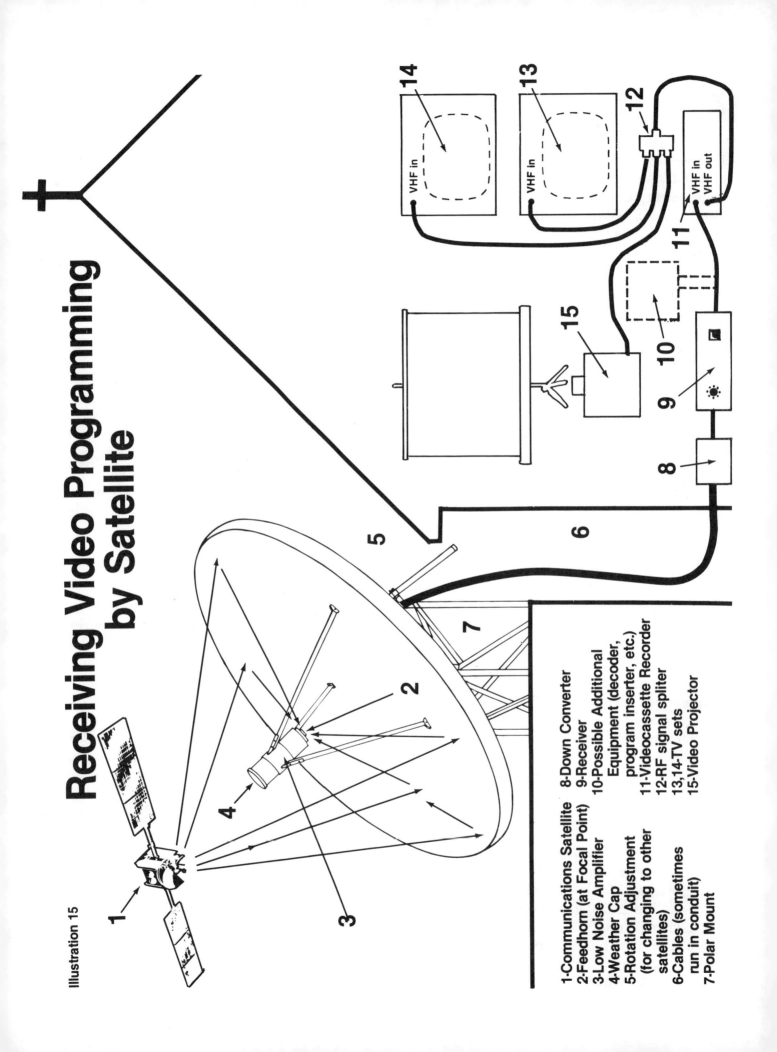

Illustration 15

Low noise amplifiers are rated in degrees. The lower degree rating, the better and more costly the LNA. Though the home satellite dish industry offered a standard one-hundred-twenty-degree LNA for some time, satellite educational services have recommended one-hundred-degree LNAs or even lower ratings if decoding devices have been included in the system. (When satellite-delivered educational services are "scrambled" or encoded, a decoder is required for a clear signal.)]

6. *Receiver* [The receiver gets the signal from the LNA through a downconverter. (The downconverter processes the signal into a usable frequency range and sends it on to the receiver.) The receiver converts this information to an RF signal for a television set or recorder (see glossary). The average receiver has access to all twenty-four transponders (or channels) transmitted from a satellite. Since half of these signals are on a different polarity—some odd and some even—a method of changing polarity is necessary or the receiver will only be capable of twelve-channel reception. Make sure your receiver has an *electronic polarizing device*. Otherwise, you will have to go out to the dish and physically turn a piece of equipment to reverse polarity.

    Once a receiver is properly installed, you will be able to change to all twenty-four channels of a satellite by turning a knob similar to a television timer. Remote control—wired and wireless—is also available.

    If you also plan to use your dish for providing a religious or family network to a local cable system, a broadcast-quality receiver and a large dish are likely requirements.]

7. *Tracking package* [Should you plan to leave your dish on one satellite, you do not need a tracking package. A tracker is a motorized device for moving the dish from focusing on one satellite to focus on a different satellite. An occasional move can be accomplished with a simple hand crank. If you will be moving your dish frequently, however, the tracker is recommended highly. Some trackers are programmable, allowing you to change from satellite to satellite on command from a remote control.]

8. *Cable/installation* [The number of cables required for a dish installation and complexity of installation vary widely. Generally speaking, the fewer number of cables required between the dish and the receiver inside your building, the better. Make this comparison when shopping.]

    [Also, check to see if installation is included in the sales price. How much installation material is included in this price? Is the concrete footing provided by the installer? Under one hundred feet is the recommended distance between dish and the receiver. At far greater distances, costly modifications may be required during the installation for you to get an optimum picture.]

9. *Warranty/service* [Warranties are greatly different within the satellite dish industry. Compare length of warranties as well as coverage. Most important, how quickly can you get service if there is a breakdown? Will the company loan equipment to you during repair of your equipment?]

[For more detailed information, all of the major components of a satellite-receiving system are defined in the glossary.]

The information given above on pieces of video equipment for various education involvements is not intended to be all-inclusive or exhaustive. Instead, key features have been highlighted to provide you with measuring devices when doing comparison shopping. A basic understanding of these features will enable you to evaluate responses from various dealers and to select the best equipment values for your needs.

Note

1. One excellent source of video equipment descriptions and list prices is the Audio Visual Equipment Directory published by NAVA, the International Communication Industries Association, ICIA. This annual publication is probably available at your local library or audiovisual dealer.

5
Selecting Video Equipment for Use in Cablecasting/Broadcasting

[Note: This chapter centers on cablecasting and, to some degree, on low-power television broadcasting. Though principles are applicable to full-power television, references will be limited to cable or LPTV due to the currently greater opportunity.]

"What I Have Learned the Hard Way About Selecting Video Equipment for Cablecasting/Broadcasting" might be a more appropriate title for this chapter. That has been the testimony of so many early users of cable television. Church leaders have found no shortage of literature, but much of it has been slanted toward a particular brand. Sales representatives have been eager to put a package of *their* equipment together for you. In an effort to provide a price lower than the competitor, however, some have eliminated a piece of needed equipment and offered it only as an option. Or they have not included several hundred dollars worth of cables and connectors, "assuming you would know" that these items were needed in the package. Though no maliciousness was intended by these individuals, a church leader who had no video background has often found himself in the embarrassing circumstance of asking for more money even before the cablecasting ministry began.

Good news! There are now simplified listings of suggested equipment which do not require a television engineer's license to understand them. Moreover, prices have fallen to the point of being affordable to most churches. (One pastor recently commented on equipment prices: "When we started broadcasting our worship services a few years ago, we paid more for one camera than the entire package costs today!")

As mentioned in chapter 4, you do not have to purchase all of your equipment at one time as long as selected items will function in the enlarged system. Some church leaders have purchased a three-tube camera of broadcast quality, a three-quarter-inch videocassette recorder, a portable lighting kit, and a microphone to begin their ministry. If you have access to an editing system, even at an hourly rate, some single camera productions can be produced effectively. One benefit of the approach is the valuable "hands-on" experience it provides in video before an entire system is purchased for the church. You may discover a preference for features not envisioned originally. On the other hand, many churches want to make a single financial expenditure, and you will need to know the "bottom line" of the complete package.

(Before acquiring a video system, check local availability of equipment. You may not have to purchase any hardware to begin your cable/LPTV involvement. A number of cable companies have equipment for loan. Many of these companies have in-house studios, too. Furthermore, well-equipped colleges and technical schools are looking for video projects to train their students. Your cable or low-power television program offers an ideal laboratory experience.)

When assembling a video production package, three types of equipment are necessary: (1) video, (2) sound and (3) lighting. Comments will be divided into those three categories.

Video Equipment

As you recall from chapter 4, the foremost question about selection is: "What do I want to do with the equipment?" Having answered this question, the explanations given below will be more helpful to you.

In an effort to support more local churches entering cablecasting or broadcasting ministries, the ACTS Satellite Network recently prepared a basic, generic equipment package. This package is a useful guide for choosing components and doing comparison shopping. Churches may also use this listing as a master plan for building a system in stages. Numbers in parentheses indicate the need for multiple units in this basic package:

Basic Video Equipment for Production

1. Camera System:
   camera body (2)
   zoom lens (2)
   rear lens control (2)
   EFP viewfinder (2) [see glossary]
   studio viewfinder (2)
   remote control unit (2)
2. Camera Support System:
   tripod (2)
   head (2)
   wheels/dolly (2)
3. Video Control System:
   switcher/special-effects generator/sync generator
   color program monitor
   dual black-and-white monitor
4. Graphics System:
   key camera
   stand for key camera
   character generator
   dual monitors
5. Video Recording System:
   videocassette recorder (¾")
6. Studio Accessories:
   intercom headsets (three)
   test charts
7. Cables and Connectors:
   complete wiring harness
8. Engineering System:
   waveform monitor/vectorscope
   dual rack mount
   routing switcher
   black-and-white monitor
9. Equipment Rack:
   custom-built or stock (see illustration 16)

The following are my own explanatory comments on the ACTS listing:

1. Camera System—Unlike the minimal requirements for educational video in chapter 4, cameras included in a cablecast/broadcast video system must have certain features. A minimum of two cameras is suggested for reducing or even eliminating editing and for providing variety in your program. Cameras must be compatible and usable in a unified system. Each camera should have an external camera control unit which can be mounted in a rack or on a shelf near other control equipment. The units must accept an external sync source so that all equipment being used will be synchronized, thus producing a usable signal. Cable to the cameras should include wiring for an intercom system for use by the director, camera operators, and other technical personnel. The camera ought to have a zoom lens, preferably with a tripod-mounted control cable. For EFP (Electronic Field Production—away-from-the-studio) work, the lens should be motor driven and controlled by a switch near the lens for operator convenience. A large viewfinder of approximately five inches for studio use and a smaller viewfinder for EFP use are needed for the camera.

Three-tube cameras are preferable to single-tube units. A prism optics system is suggested for conveying light to the camera's pickup tubes from the lens. (Some cameras use mirrors rather than a prism.) An automatic iris is important. (See the glossary.)

Other comparison features to look for are:

• *Methods of white and black balancing* [Automatic balancing is one option.]

• *Portability* [You should be able to convert at least one camera for use in the field. Be certain this camera can be operated on battery power, probably supplied from the portable videocassette recorder. Include a *shoulder mount* for carrying the camera and the small viewfinder mentioned earlier in the chapter. A sturdy carrying case will help protect your investment. A *portable AC adapter* is another valuable accessory, saving batteries on sites with electricity and prolonging recording time capability.]

Control Rack for Video Production System

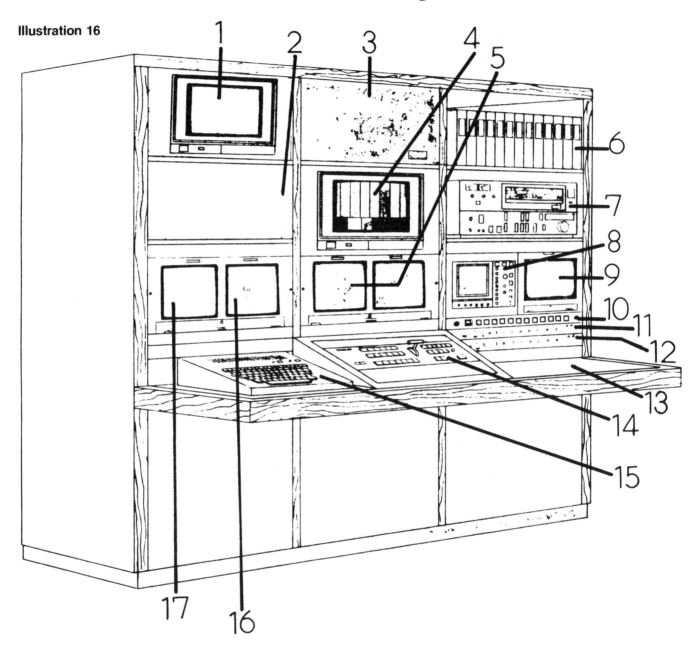

Illustration 16

1. black and white monitor for audio system
2. future expansion space
3. audio monitor (speaker)
4. 13" color program monitor
5. 9" monitors for use with switcher
6. videocassette storage
7. ¾" videocassette recorder
8. waveform monitor/vectorscope
9. 9" monitor for routing switcher
10. routing switcher
11. remote control unit for camera #1
12. remote control unit for camera #2
13. future expansion space
14. switcher/special-effects generator
15. character generator
16. 9" character generator preview monitor
17. 9" character generator program monitor

(drawing courtesy of ACTS Satellite Network)

- *Signal-to-Noise Ratio* [The suggested ratio is fifty-two decibels (db) or better.]
- *Lines of Resolution* [The greater the number of lines of resolution, the better picture you may expect with your camera.]
- *Adjustments/Simplicity* [With the wide range of cameras which are simple to operate, choose one which requires few operator adjustments and features easily accessible controls.]

2. Camera Support System—As emphasized in an earlier chapter, a quality *tripod* and *tripod head* are essential to good work. Jerky movements caused by unstable tripods or poor heads will cause even an expensive camera to produce unacceptable pictures. Use a *fluid head* rather than a *friction head*, if possible. (See glossary.) The tripod ought to have wheels or fit into a rolling dolly attachment.

3. Video Control System—Plan for a *switcher/ special-effects generator (SEG)* to serve your needs now and for the foreseeable future. For instance, purchase a unit with six or more video inputs even if you have less equipment. Expect the unit to do at least basic transitions between cameras such as fades and several wipe patterns. (See glossary.) Check to see that the switcher/SEG has an internal sync generator or will accept one. A sync control is crucial to the overall system. A minimum of three monitors is needed: one color program monitor which actually shows what is being recorded or cablecast/broadcast and two black-and-white (or color) monitors for receiving the camera signals and previewing shots before actually switching. [Please note: unlike educational video which can use television sets effectively, production systems require true monitors.]

4. Graphics System—A *key camera* is an inexpensive, black-and-white unit used for superimposing graphics over the television picture. It is mounted onto a copystand. Material to be superimposed is usually black and white with a high contrast. With a key camera, logos and other artwork can be included in your creative program.

The *character generator* enables you to superimpose alphanumeric characters onto the video picture in various colors. Prices range according to several factors, including amount of storage capability (usually called "pages"). Two *monitors* are needed: (1) to preview character generator copy and (2) to view that which is being inserted into the program.

5. Recording System—The *three-quarter-inch videocassette recorder* is a primary element in your production system. Choose a good one! If the recorder is to be mounted in a rack, purchase a front-loading VCR. If an editing system is envisioned for the future, you may wish to purchase a VCR which can dually serve as the source machine in such a setup as well as your program recorder.

[Three-quarter-inch recorders are used by the vast majority of church cablecasters/ broadcasters. These reasonably priced VCRs deliver a superior signal to regular half-inch recorders: VHS and Beta. The newer high-speed, broadcast quality half-inch recorder/camera combinations are considerably more expensive and require special playback equipment. One-inch reel-to-reel video recorders deliver the best signal, but the cost is prohibitive to many churches.

Another possibility: some cable companies may allow the use of regular VHS or Beta equipment, either with camera and recorder or with the consumer-type camera/recorder combination. (Half-inch editing systems are available for these units, too.) *Do not purchase* this type of equipment, however, until you have compared picture quality and checked with the cable company. Some cable companies do not allow regular half-inch equipment. And Federal Communications Commission regulations are subject to change.

For additional information on VCRs, see chapter 4.]

6. Studio Accessories—*Intercom headsets* are required for a production system. The best type are those which plug directly into the camera and control board. Signals from the intercoms are then carried on the camera cables. *Test charts*—posterettes with printed test patterns—are used to determine the need for camera adjustments.

7. Cables and Connectors—Stipulate that complete wiring is to be included in any system price quotation. If not, you will be looking for at least several hundred additional dollars to complete your installation.

8. Engineering System—To determine if cameras are balanced and delivering an optimum signal as well as to diagnose other signal problems, you need test equipment. A *waveform monitor* and a *vectorscope* (or a combination unit) will be essential to maintain the quality required for cablecasting/broadcasting.

Stipulating that these units be rack mountable enables you to install them with other control equipment. A *routing switcher* equips you to switch audio and video signals between various pieces of equipment.

9. Equipment Rack—All of your control equipment—character generator, switcher/SEG, monitors, test equipment, routing switcher, etc.—must be housed in some type of storage unit. Standard nineteen-inch-wide steel racks are available but tend to be quite costly. Several companies prefabricate units out of less expensive material such as chipboard. (See illustration.) Units may also be constructed locally.

With careful, comparative shopping, all of the equipment listed above, including the laminated chipboard control rack, can be secured for about twenty-five-thousand dollars in a *do-it-yourself installation. [Note: the list price of this equipment far exceeds that amount. However, never pay list price for video equipment. If the dealer will not sell below list, it is time to check with a different dealer!]*

Audio Equipment

Audio is often neglected when preparing for cablecasting/broadcasting. Yet poor sound quality will significantly lessen the impact of your production. Television viewers expect sophistication in sound as evidenced by the brisk sales of stereo televisions, stereo VCRs, and digital audio equipment.

As in video equipment, the ACTS Satellite Network has designed an audio package for basic auditorium configuration. It is a complete system which does not require "feeds" from the existing auditorium's sound system. You may not find it necessary to install an entirely new system if your sound equipment is adequate. However, you *will* want to have a separate audio mixer for television which receives sound prior to any modification from a house mixer. In other words, sound control for television is not the same as for in-house. To rely on a feed from the house system is a mistake. If you were to purchase an entire audio system, this would be a basic configuration:

Basic Audio Equipment for Video Production in a Church Auditorium

1. Microphones:
   cardioid microphones (four)
   twenty-five-foot cable with connectors (five)
   PZM phantom-powered microphones (three) (with one-hundred-foot light grey cable and connectors)
2. Microphone Stands and Booms:
   pulpit mount with flexible "gooseneck," rigid sections, and mounting flange (one)
   model UMS 101 floor stand or equivalent (one)
   model UDS 101 desk stand or equivalent (one)
3. Portable Stage Input and Cables:
   six-input PSI with labeling to match inputs on boxes and connector ends, one hundred feet long (two) connecting cable thirty feet long from mixer line out to VTR audio in (one).
4. Audio Mixer:
   twelve-input audio mixer with power amps (one)
5. Monitor System:
   studio monitor (two-way) (one)
   connecting cable thirty feet long with connectors (one)
   aura-one 5C (one)
   connecting cable three feet long with connectors (one)
6. Closed Circuit TV System (important for audio operator to see the "live" action):
   black-and-white TV camera with lens (one)
   camera mount (one)
   camera cable to monitor (fifty feet)

fifteen-inch black-and-white TV monitor (one)

Since this is not intended to be a technical volume, an explanation will not be given for each piece listed above. They are standard audio components. Virtually any audio dealer or even an audiophile in your church can give a full explanation, if you desire.

Approximate cost for the complete audio system, including a console for the mixer, is four thousand dollars for a *do-it-yourself installation*.

Lighting Equipment

Lighting required for television depends largely on the location you select for recording. Ceiling height, room size, and types of programming will influence your lighting requirements. Lighting a studio will obviously vary from lighting most church sanctuaries. Desiring to light two scenes simultaneously rather than one focal point is another variable.

An array of features and lamps is available once you determine what you want to accomplish with lighting. For example, consider this lighting package designed by the Radio and Television Commission of the Southern Baptist Convention.[1] It serves a church with auditorium dimensions not exceeding sixty feet in length, forty-five feet in width, and thirty-five feet from floor to ceiling:

- thirteen theatrical/television-type lighting fixtures
- a twelve-channel master control unit
- a portable, six-channel dimmer
- cables and connectors
- a control console

Approximate cost is forty-five hundred dollars. This do-it-yourself installation does include in the cost projections any expenditures for additional power supplies to accommodate the system. An additional 12,500 watts of power is required for the lighting fixtures/lamps alone. With this sample system, several emphasis areas can be illuminated easily.

In searching for the right lighting package to meet your needs, keep these considerations in mind:

- *fixture placement* [The vertical angle of fixture placement should be high enough to avoid blinding the speaker while low enough to eliminate shadows around the eyes and chin. This is approximately a thirty-degree angle.]
- *overall lighting effect* [The light level should be balanced, not punctuated with "hot" spots.]
- *color temperature* [Television lighting ought to be in the range of 2900° to 3200° Kelvin. (See glossary and appendix A.) Dominant lighting with other color temperatures will distort the picture.
- *filtering for RF interference* [Some dimming systems cause video equipment to pick up RF (radio frequency) signals in electrical wiring because they are not properly filtered. An entire video program can be ruined if lighting controls lack filtering. For instance, a loud buzzing will be recorded on the audio track each time lighting levels are changed in the production.
- *power surges* [Check to see how much power surge a system can handle. This is particularly important in areas affected by frequent power irregularities.]
- *fixture types* [Selection of fixtures—such as *scoop, fresnel, ellipsoidal,* and *mini ellipsoidal*—will depend on lighting requirements. (See illustration 17.) Intensity, coverage area, and pattern of light desired are some of the determining factors. (See illustration 18.) Since most fixtures accept lamps of various wattages, lamp selection will also be influenced by lighting requirements.]
- *Camera requirements* [Your camera will operate at its best when the subject is illuminated to a certain light level. Insist that any system being considered delivers this intensity of light.]

As you can see, effective lighting is a matter of desired effect, personal taste, technical requirements, and individual locales. It can be a video production's best friend or its worst enemy.

[Note: Many local utility companies offer free or inexpensive lighting consultations. If not, they can refer you to other local sources.]

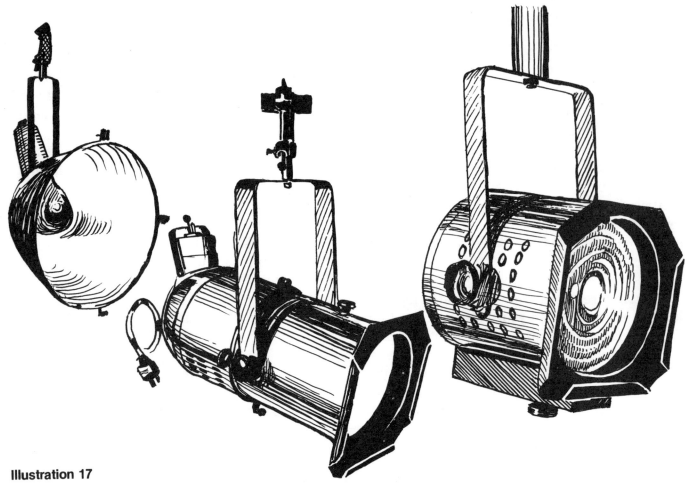

Illustration 17

Types of studio lights (left to right): scoop, ellipsoidal, and Fresnel.

Illustration 18   **Example of portable lighting kit**

Other Equipment Considerations—A seemingly unending list of equipment pieces could be proposed for a video production package. However, three items not specified in the video equipment section ought to be mentioned as possible requirements:

1. *Time Base Corrector (TBC)*—A TBC corrects stability errors in the time base of a tape during playback. One example of a problem in time base is when a videotape stretches, thus lengthening it. Though the tape is now longer, there is no additional content. The time base is incorrect since it takes longer for the tape to pass through the machine. Variances in time base may be found in different video signal sources, too.

A TBC has been described as being like a large coffee pot. You can pour in liquid at different speeds and intensities, but it comes out of the spout in an even flow. Though you can "pour" signals into a TBC at varying rates and intensities, they come out in a smooth, even flow. Therefore, a TBC is needed when blending two video sources into one in an editing situation, such as superimposing a logo or lettering over a picture or fading from one VCR signal to another VCR.

Some cable companies or low-power television stations require you to use a TBC even though they may run your tape through a TBC before airing.

2. *Editing Package*—If you are fortunate enough to have access to an editor, even if you have to pay a reasonable hourly rate, you are probably not concerned about editing. However, if you cannot edit at all, everything must be done in "real time"—as it happens. A mistake requires starting from the beginning again or chancing a picture breakup in the final product.

3. *Portable Recorder*—Time base correctors and editors are rather expensive. You may wish to project their acquisition at a later date. But, purchase of a portable videocassette recorder is less costly.

Remote settings are sometimes ideal for accomplishing your programming purpose. With your portable recorder and a camera in the EFP configuration, any setting is within reach.

Getting Started

Numerous resource persons in your community or at least in your denomination would be happy to assist you in formulating the best video production package for your church, whether it will be a one-time purchase or a multistage acquisition.

These persons will be better able to meet your requests if you know what you want to accomplish, how much money you can spend, and when you plan to begin production.

Best wishes as you contemplate this exciting video ministry involvement.

Note

1. The Southern Baptist Radio and Television Commission is the world's largest producer of public service programming for radio and television. In addition, the Commission administers the ACTS Satellite Network, Inc., a family and religious television network which includes programs from most of the major mainline Christian denominations.

Appendix A:
How Video Works

Church leaders benefit from a basic nontechnical understanding of how video works. Evaluating cameras and recorders for purchase is easier when you know the significance of their key features. The importance of certain maintenance requirements will be recognized readily. And the quality of productions will likely improve as you comprehend how the picture is made, stored, and reproduced by video equipment.

Before explaining the video process, one of the main elements ought to be emphasized: *light*.

Light is the key to video. All video (recording and playback) is based on light. Poor lighting for taping negatively impacts the entire production.

Prior to any video recording, the camera is adjusted to correctly sense "white light." ("White light" is actually light in the full range of the color spectrum.) This adjustment, called "white balancing," may require the touch of one button or adjustment of several controls. Many cameras have automatic white balancing.

The process of white balancing involves focusing the camera on a white surface (poster, sheet of paper, object—anything white) and "informing" the camera that the image being received is white. Once white is "recognized," all colors can be delineated properly.

White balancing is required each time a camera is moved into a new light environment. Various light sources produce different *color temperatures* which are measured in *degrees Kelvin*. (Color temperature is the particular mix of colors making up white.) A video picture which distorts color probably reveals that the camera is not properly white balanced for the environment. For instance, incandescent lights are more "reddish white" and fluorescent lights are "bluish." Some of the common color temperatures are:

2000° Kelvin—normal incandescent lighting
3200° Kelvin—quartz and incandescent studio lights
4800° Kelvin—fluorescent light
5000° Kelvin—cloudy day
7000° Kelvin—cloudless day (approximate)

As you can see, light is the key to accurate video recording and reproduction. As the video process is explained below, light will be the common denominator:

The first step in video processing is that the video camera pictures (or "sees") an object as reflected light. Light (or radiated energy) passes through the camera lens and is focused onto a light-sensitive surface of the camera pickup tube, sometimes called the "target area." In three-tube cameras, the light image is split into three parts before reaching the pickup tubes. This splitting is accomplished by a prism (preferable) or a set of mirrors. Each of the tubes has particular sensitivity to one of the primary colors making up the television picture: red, green, and blue.

Once the light reaches the target area of the tube (or tubes), the image is momentarily retained on the surface. (See illustration 19.) An electron gun at the opposite end of the pickup tube generates a beam which scans the light-sensitive target area. This scanning takes place in a cycle of two passes. Each pass draws 262.5 parallel lines as the electron beam moves left to right, from top to bottom. On the second top-to-bottom pass of the electron beam, another 262.5 parallel horizontal lines are drawn between the 262.5 lines of the original pass. Each pass is called a *field*, with the two complete passes of a cycle being called a *frame*. This frame contains *525 lines* composed of thousands of dots *(or pixels)*.

An entire frame is required to form one recog-

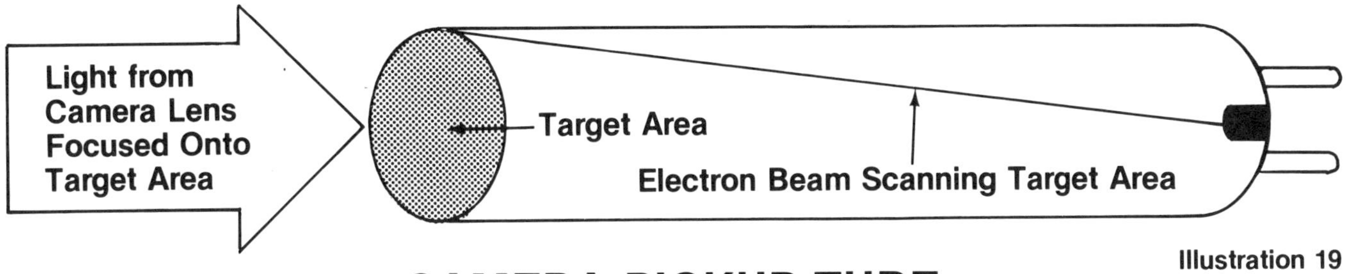

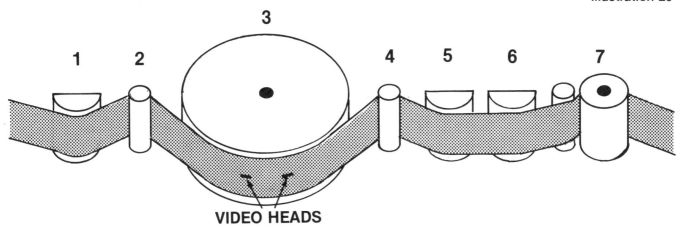

CAMERA PICKUP TUBE

Illustration 19

Components Which Videotape Passes in Record and Playback Modes

Illustration 20

1. Erase Head removes all stored signals in the record mode and does not function in playback.

2,4. Tape Guides properly position the videotape in the recorder, including the path around the rotating video head drum.

3. Video Head Drum rotates clockwise with video heads on the drum, recording signals onto videotape in the record mode and retrieving signals from the videotape in the playback mode. The tape passes over the drum at a slant, creating "stripes" of video signal on the tape.

5. Audio Head records sound onto videotape in the same manner as an audio recorder and retrieves the sound signal in playback.

6. Control Track Head records information onto the videotape for synchronizing sound, picture, and speed in playback.

7. Capstan rotates, pressing the videotape against the rubber pinch roller. This "sandwich effect" pulls the tape through the recorder at the speed governed by the synchronization signals in the record mode and the control track in the playback mode.

nizable picture. Though only one half of a picture is produced with each pass of a field, your eye never delineates this fact. Since the human eye retains an image for one fifteenth (1/15) of a second and the two passes together only take one thirtieth (1/30) of a second, the images blend together.

As mentioned earlier, the two passes of an electron beam in a camera pickup tube create a total of 525 lines. Hence, television in the United States and several other countries is said to have *525 lines of resolution*. This 525-line measurement was agreed upon by the National Television Standards Committee (NTSC), an engineering advisory group to the Federal Communications Commission.

[Note: equipment sold for use in this country meets the NTSC standard. Since many other countries use other standards—PAL or SECAM—a change of tapes is not always possible. For instance, if you wanted to show a videotape sent from a missionary in France, you would need to know if his videocassette recorder was on the NTSC standard. If he purchased his machine "off the shelf" in France, it would likely be on the SECAM standard of 625 lines of resolution. (See glossary.) Even though he sent a half-inch VHS tape and you had a VHS recorder, the tape would not play properly.]

Understanding the NTSC 525-line standard is important when selecting video equipment. If a videocassette recorder or television set will only accept a certain number of lines of resolution, purchasing a camera with significantly greater resolution capacity is not money well spent.

The second step in the video process involves the reaction of the electron beam as it scans the target area of the camera pickup tube. Various intensities of light being retained on the pickup tube cause differing reactions for the scanning beam. These reactions to light intensity are converted into electrical energy.

[An important note: some of the latest video cameras do not use the same process for "capturing" reflected light on an object as described in steps one and two. Instead of a camera pickup tube with target area and electron gun, they are equipped with a charged coupled device (CCD). A CCD is a light-sensitive, integrated circuit. Light passing through the camera lens is focused onto this CCD which translates it into electrical energy. Elimination of the pickup tube can reduce the size and weight of cameras.]

In the third step of the video process, an image in the form of electrical energy is stored on magnetic tape. This storage method is similar to that used for producing audiocassettes. In fact, the audio portion of a videotape is recorded in an identical manner to that of an audiotape.

As the videotape passes through the recorder which is now in the "record" mode, the *erase head* removes any signal which may already be on the tape. The erase head is an electromagnetic device which "scrambles" existing magnetic patterns. (See illustration 20.)

The tape next moves past the *video record heads*. These heads are electromagnetic instruments. A close inspection reveals a "U-shaped" device not unlike a regular electromagnet. (See illustration 21.) It is important that spacing between the two poles remain dirt free for proper recording and playback. When this space becomes filled, the condition is called "fouled heads."

Video heads rotate horizontally on a circular drum. The video signals, in the form of electrical energy, are placed onto the tape as magnetic impulses in long, parallel stripes, each stripe containing *262.5 lines* or a *field*. (See illustration 22.) Two of these invisible, magnetic stripes of information contain one *frame* or a complete video picture of 525 lines.

The videotape continues past the audio record/playback head where audio information is stored on one or two channels on the edge of the tape.

Finally passing the *control track record/playback head*, information is recorded onto the control track area of the tape for assuring that all parts of the signal—audio and video—will be synchronized for later playback. The control track serves the same function as sprocket holes on movie film. Instead of holes being placed in the tape so that rotating sprocket heads pull it through a recorder, videotape is pulled through a recorder by a rotating spindle *(capstan)* pressing the tape against a *rubber pinch roller*. The speed

Closeup of Video Recording Heads
(photo by R. Chip Turner)

Illustration 21

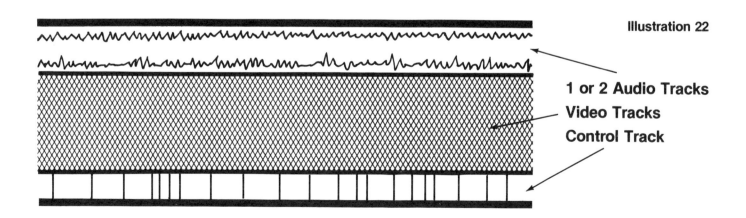

Illustration 22

1 or 2 Audio Tracks
Video Tracks
Control Track

Signals on a Videotape

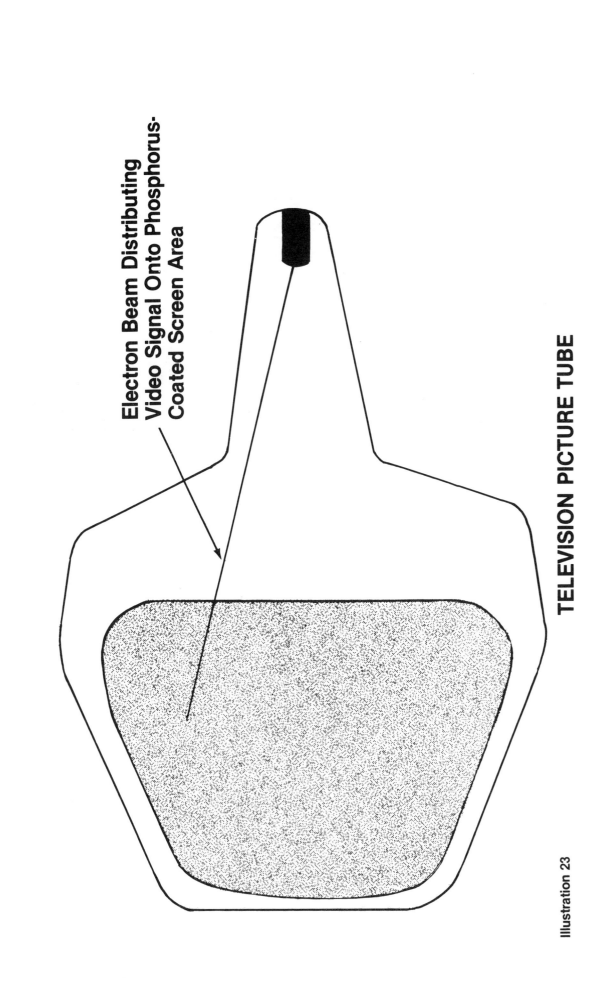

TELEVISION PICTURE TUBE

Illustration 23

Appendix A: How Video Works

of a capstan's rotation is determined by the control track.

Now all of the picture and sound signals are stored on magnetic videotape.

Placing your recorder in the "play" mode reverses the recording process. Where there are record *and* playback heads, playback heads function now. Some heads, however, must serve in dual capacities on less-expensive recorders.

The control track regulates speed of the tape being pulled through the VCR as the rotating video heads retrieve the stripes of magnetically stored data, turning it into electrical energy. Audio heads pick up the tracks of sound data.

Audio and video signals as electrical energy pass through an RF modulator to convert this information into a radio frequency (RF) recognized by a television set as a channel. (Signals are also available as "audio out" and "video out" on some videocassette recorders. The "raw" signal of "video out" can only be used by a monitor since it has not been modulated into a TV channel frequency.)

Once the signal reaches a television set, audio is processed through an amplifier and on to the speaker. Video, in the form of electrical energy, reaches an electron gun (or guns) at the rear of the picture tube. (See illustration 23.) This electron gun sends out a beam to scan the picture tube, distributing this electrical signal onto the surface of the picture tube. Since the face of the picture tube is coated with a phosphorus-like material, it "glows" in proportion to the strength of the electrical energy received, thus forming a video picture with intensities of light.

[As in changes with camera technology which offer a charge-coupled device (CCD) instead of a camera pickup tube in some models, standard vacuum picture tubes are not the only technology available for reproducing video pictures. Flat field video screens are available, making wristwatch television pictures a reality. Watch for further refinements in this area.]

You can now see how important light is to the video process. A video picture begins as *reflected light*, is changed into *electrical energy*, stored as *magnetic energy*, retrieved as *electrical energy*, and *projected as light*.

Appendix B:
Seventy-Five Programming Ideas for Local Cable/LPTV Productions

Surveys have proven that targeted, locally produced programming has appeal to viewers. Yet merely being on television does not guarantee an audience. A potential audience must be identified, kept in mind during scripting and production, and informed prior to airing of the program.

The *best* sources of local programming ideas are you, your fellow church members, and other community citizens. Ideas will begin to flow as you assess the community. *What makes your community unique? What activities are popular? What are the ongoing problems?* Answers to these questions will help analyze potential target audiences and spark additional ideas.

Many of the suggestions below are the result of church leaders reflecting upon needs and interests in their communities which may be addressed via television. The variety indicates a desire to minister to the whole person while building an audience for more overtly evangelistic programs.

These topics are simply thought starters awaiting your creative refinement, based on knowledge of your community. Program identifications are working titles, not suggestions for final program designations:

(1) Regular Worship Service—When a church leader thinks of using television in the church's ministry, cablecasting or broadcasting a regular worship service frequently comes to mind. There is no doubt that such programs are meeting needs of a community segment, especially the homebound. Some church leaders are deciding that they also wish to produce another type of program to meet recognized needs of certain target groups which are not watching the worship service.

[Note: to realize optimum effectiveness from a televised worship service requires planning with the viewers in mind. While remembering the viewers, your production approach must not make those present in the sanctuary feel they are just a studio audience for a television program. Attention can be focused on television viewers in several ways without the knowledge of those present: (1) a personalized introduction by the pastor or a staff minister at the beginning of the program, (2) a segment during the offertory, (3) an opportunity to call in for personal counseling, and (4) a word at the conclusion of the service. These personal touches can be prerecorded and inserted at the appropriate points.]

(2) Today's Teenage Issues—Enlist one or more attractive, fluent youth to co-host this program with the pastor, youth minister, or volunteer leader. Choose topics of interest to local teenagers—peer pressure, drugs, parental relationships, and so on. (A key to audience building will be the selected topics. Do not assume you know the subjects of interest to teens. Ask them!)

(3) Bible Character Interviews—Take viewers back to biblical times as a way of teaching scriptural truths. Dialogue can center on an accounting of biblical events or reinforcing a learning experience. Characters in costume will always gain attention.

(4) Christian Book Review—Enlist your church librarian to review one or more Christian books for each episode. A local Christian book store might even be willing to sponsor this program. (At the least, the manager can have multiple copies of reviewed books available in the store.) Such a program is certain to increase readership in your local church library.

(5) Sunday School Lesson Overview—This

program can take at least two approaches: (1) provide another Bible study opportunity for area residents or (2) offer additional preparation help for Bible study teachers prior to their Sunday lesson presentations. You might even coordinate the program with other Bible study outreach ministries or training experiences for your Sunday School teachers.

(6) Children's Show—There is a shortage of good children's programming, and you have the lay people in your church who can make this positive contribution. Why not involve some of the "Bible characters" from program suggestion number 3? Have these characters tell a Bible story. You might include "today's Bible memory verse" and encourage children to look up Scriptures in their own Bibles. Offer to send a Bible to each child who does not have one.

Invite children's groups to be in the audience and guarantee yourself viewers when the show is aired—the children, their friends, parents, grandparents, and so on.

(7) Latchkey Children's Show—Scores of children are coming in from school to empty houses since both parents are employed outside the home. A program for latchkey children serves the community well. Such a project may be done in cooperation with a local youth organization such as Boy Scouts, Girl Scouts, or Camp Fire, which have all produced good materials for use with latchkey children.

(8) Tips for the Handicapped—Focus on special needs and interests of handicapped persons. Keep these individuals informed of issues facing them and ways they can positively respond to these issues.

(9) Exercise for the Handicapped—Exercise shows are popular on television, but little attention is given to exercise needs of the handicapped. Among local resource persons are physicians and physical therapists. Perhaps a physically handicapped person with good television presence can be a good host or co-host.

(10) Help for the Homebound—Sick and shut-in individuals have a number of special problems. And they are a faithful audience when you address their needs. If your church has a ministry to the homebound, one of the active participants probably has the understanding necessary to serve as a consultant or even as an on-camera personality.

(11) Christian Aerobics—With the high interest in exercise and the added audience appeal of locally originated programming, this suggestion has significant potential. If you determine that women will largely compose the audience, testimonies of successful housewives and women with careers outside the home can be interspersed with the exercises. This enlarges the number of on-camera personalities and, hence, the number of viewers.

Potential leadership for the program is probably awaiting discovery in your Young Adult Sunday School department. Though not limited to one age group or sex, this program has particular appeal to young- and median-adult women.

(12) Today's Music Feature—In your church and community there are scores of talented musicians: choirs, ensembles, soloists, and instrumentalists. Consider producing a weekly program of Christian music. If you have access to a network channel such as the American Christian Television System (ACTS), there are even opportunities each hour of the day to do two-and-a-half-minute and one-and-a-half-minute miniconcerts during programming breaks for local spot insertion.

(13) Tips for Volunteer Church Music Directors—This is a service to churches who have volunteer music directors without the benefit of formal training. Your music minister, paid or volunteer, can host such a program. Another "slant" is to offer tips for all volunteers who direct preschool and children's choirs. Or you can target volunteers who lead music for Sunday School departments and other church organizations.

(14) Your Health Care—Produce a show which helps people learn how to stay healthier by taking vitamins, eating natural foods, and properly cooking foods. Invite nutritionists, health care professionals, dietitians, and others to be guests on the program. Help viewers learn proper food preparation and eating habits. Give attention to people with restricted diets, also. Share recipes each time for a special diet which can be enjoyed by every viewer.

(15) Ask the Minister—Write-in and call-in radio and television programs are quite popular, commanding large audiences. This approach allows inquirers to ask the minister about spiritual and personal problems, biblical questions, and so on.

[One caution: seasoned cable "veterans" suggest you ask viewers to write in rather than call in. Some weeks do not yield enough telephone callers to sustain the program. On other occasions, callers may all gravitate to one subject and offer little help to other viewers. Keep responses balanced in favor of the larger audience.]

(16) Ask the Counselor—Similar to suggestion number 15, this program involves other trained Christian counselors with specialties such as marriage and family. The program enables Christian leaders in your church to share their talents with the community. And these professionals become known as resource persons to a broader audience which may later need their services.

(17) Comparative Theology—Your church can coordinate this feature of various area ministers sharing theological distinctives of their faiths. Such a program fosters greater understanding and appreciation for area churches. One prerequisite of participants should be their willingness to be positive as they highlight similarities of and differences with other denominations.

(18) Christian Youth Quiz Bowl—This program features youth groups from area churches who compete in four-person teams (or panels) for overall winner. Questions are drawn from Bible knowledge as well as general knowledge. An audience of area church members is guaranteed, especially during the weeks when their young people are featured on the quiz bowl.

(19) Denominational Distinctives—Somewhat similar to idea number 17, this program highlights positive happenings and unique projects of the denominations more than comparing theology. Many people are interested in knowing about various denominations. Include current mission endeavors, strategies or goals, and other distinctives. Center on the denomination's activities in the local area.

(20) Focus on Child Care—One of your experienced workers, along with periodic guests, offers tips on child care. An easily recognized target audience is parents of newborns. Major on the practical aspects of child care as learned through experience with one's own children and children ministered to in the child-care ministry of your church. This program offers you another chance to show the community your church really cares for parents and young children.

(21) Living with Teens—Enlist the youth minister or youth Sunday School leader to co-host this program. Involve a variety of parents of current teenagers in a sharing experience of their pilgrimages. Also invite Christian teachers, coaches, and administrators of local junior and senior high schools to offer their input. Include teenage guests as well. Offer an opportunity for viewers to write or call in topics of interest for future segments.

(22) Ethics: the Christian Perspective—This program centers on current ethical issues, particularly in the fields of law and medicine. Christian doctors, nurses, lawyers, judges, and law enforcement officers are just some of the possible persons you can involve, at least as periodic program guests.

(23) Christian Talk Show—Include as your guests those in the community who are making a positive impact on the lives of others. (When local people are featured, local people watch the program!)

Out-of-town guest leaders for local church events offer another resource pool for the show.

(24) Church Bulletin Board—List the regular and special activities of your church. Some cable channels are dedicated to such announcements. In smaller cable markets, managers are eager to get this type of news to fill their channel. Take advantage of the service. Participation requires no financial expenditure!

If you have access to time on a family/religious network, regularly update the community regarding your schedule of events. You may want to share time with all area churches, thus assuring an ongoing supply of news bits.

(25) Job-a-thon—As a public service to the community, offer a feature or a static video display of

employment opportunities in the area. Such a service is an excellent way of expressing genuine concern in the community and promoting goodwill.

(26) Volunteer Opportunities—Similar to number 25, this program or static video display is a "job board" listing opportunities for volunteers in your area. You can expect enthusiastic support from local civic organizations and agencies.

(27) Facing Tomorrow: a Look at Retirement—With the percentage of senior adults on the increase, you are offering a public service with a built-in audience. Target audiences include the retired and those facing retirement in a few years.

Always of benefit is financial planning help. Show senior adults with limited incomes how they can make the most of their resources. Offer financial planning advice to those facing retirement. Local agencies, government offices, and financial institutions are just three of the many sources of program guests. Successful retired persons add a note of authority to the program.

(28) The Senior Scene—This program is designed to inform senior adults of what is available locally for them to do. Major on free and inexpensive activities so as to include help for the largest possible audience. The program offers a superb opportunity to showcase your church's senior adult activities and ministries. Maybe you can enlist one of your senior adults as co-host.

[Note: Senior adults are also an excellent source of television crew members for this and other programs. Large and small churches are heavily dependent on senior adults to operate their television ministries.]

(29) Wills, Trusts, and Insurance Made Simple—Though of particular interest to senior adults, this program will have a broader audience. Since laws vary from state to state, a local program has more potential value than a network feature which must use a general approach. Call upon lawyers, financial advisors, investors, and insurance salespersons to help you.

(30) A Widow's World—Deal with unique problems of widows and widowers on this show. Topics like "dealing with grief," "living alone," "medical problems," "changes in social life," and "financial adjustments" are just starter ideas. Feature local ministers, physicians, and counselors as well as successful widows and widowers.

(31) The Minister Continuing to Study—Through the local ministerial alliance, a college, seminary, or seminary-level continuing education program, offer local ministers the chance of staying current in their studies. This continuing education opportunity is helpful to those unable to do graduate work as well as to seminary-trained individuals. In addition to theological topics, include such diverse studies as "Using Personal Computers in My Sermon Preparation" and "Tax Preparation for Ministers." Think of the resource persons in the ministerial ranks and secular professions!

(32) The Christian Leader—This religious education curriculum for volunteers in the local church has real potential for helping Bible teachers, organizational leaders, and directors sharpen their skills. Such a program gives you an additional chance to train leadership beyond the brief "at-church" time. In addition, you can make a contribution to the religious education ministries of other churches whose leaders benefit from your cablecast/broadcast.

(33) Adventures in Education—This continuing education program is for the general public. Investigate possibilities of using faculty members from local colleges and trade schools to offer organized course work. In some cases, credit may even be offered to those completing the courses.

Here is one example: Christian colleges may make faculty members available "in person" or via videotape to teach Bible courses. Such a program helps people while promoting a particular institution.

Adults are becoming involved in a variety of continuing education experiences via television and in classroom settings. Their primary interests seem to be skill training as much or more than academic credit.

(34) The Churchwoman—Concentrate on issues facing today's Christian woman, both inside the church and in the workaday world. Include case histories of how Christian women can respond to non-Christians in real-life situations.

(35) Television Tutor—Enlist a teacher or

teachers in your church membership to do a few episodes or an ongoing series related to tutoring. There are several approaches, including these two:

    a. Actually offer ongoing tutoring sessions on cable. (There is a genuine need for such help.)

    b. Provide generalized help in "how to study," "how to take notes," and so on.

(36) Fifth Quarter—This show is designed to give that "something extra" to underprivileged children. Local needs will determine content, such as:

    a. Showing role models of locals who overcame their situations in life.

    b. Offering cultural experiences not available to economically underprivileged children.

    c. Sharing specialized tutoring such as English courses in areas where there are large concentrations of foreign-language groups.

(37) Religious Newscene—This program is an actual newscast covering religious developments nationally and beyond, but with an emphasis on *local*. Somewhat similar to the "community bulletin board" on some full-power broadcast stations, this program is already popular in numerous locations. Use other churches as resources as well as their denominational papers and interdenominational news services.

(38) A Christian View of the News—Offer a weekly commentary on the secular news. Content includes any implications news happenings have for the church.

(39) Local Newscast—Churches are discovering a "wide open field" with a guaranteed audience when they provide weekly secular newscasts in a community which has no television station. People *will* watch your newscast, while forgiving some technical inadequacies. Their only alternative is to watch a distant station which rarely mentions your town. As you develop credibility, you also will broaden your audience. For example, key town officials will ask for opportunities to appear on the program.

In some areas, more people watch the local weekly newscast by the church than any other program during that time slot. After all, you are addressing an instantly recognized need!

(40) Real Christians—A spin-off of a television show of similar name, this program features local Christians who serve their church and community. They effectively demonstrate the Christian life.

(41) The Corner Hobby Shop—Local crafts-artists demonstrate their skills in handicrafts, photography, art, and other hobbies. They explain how and why they became involved in particular hobbies and how local viewers can try them. Information is shared on supply sources as well as any organizations involved in the hobby.

(42) Church Sports League—In this sports-minded society, why not tape and replay highlights from local church sports leagues or even community sports leagues?

(43) High School/College Athletics Coverage—One church in a major television market with several full-power stations regularly draws the largest cable audience share when they replay high school football games from one of the local schools. This cablecast features comments by the coach and minispots about the church. In another market, a church on an ACTS cable channel carries a local college's basketball games.

You can do the same type of cablecast of a local high school or college sport with minimal equipment and all-volunteer crew members. Furthermore, you will have a guaranteed audience.

(44) My Christian Witness—This is a "how-to" program on sharing your Christian faith with others. Give demonstrations on how to make a faith-sharing visit. Offer testimonies of people who have responded to such visits.

(45) The Christian Theater—Maximize available talent in your church by sharing these individuals with the community. Include drama, puppetry, clowning, and other performing skills.

(46) Self-Improvement Courses—As a community service, enlist skillful individuals to lead seminars on recognized needs. For instance, operate a "stop smoking" or "weight loss" course. You may be surprised at the number of viewers.

(47) Prison Reach—Do you have a large county jail or even a state or federal prison nearby? Some

Appendix B: Seventy-Five Programming Possibilities for Cablecasting/LPTV

churches have encountered significant response to Bible study directed specifically to prisoners. The program can be broadened to address other spiritual and physical needs of prisoners and their families. Such a program may serve as a follow-up to actual in-prison and family visits.

(48) Homebound Bible Reach—This Bible study program addresses those unable to leave their homes. Whenever possible, the teacher uses specific names on the program of shut-ins which have been reported to the church's ministry or by telephone calls and mail of viewers. Television is an intimate medium and cablecasting allows this personal touch.

(49) Children's Value Search—Addressing the need for teaching values to children, each program covers a different aspect. Concrete examples in children's terms are used, including true-life situations of well-known Bible characters. (Several helpful books offer ample case histories for idea starters.)

(50) The Storyteller—Every church has one or more persons skilled in storytelling, both contemporary and biblical. Videotape some of these stories as miniprograms, programming breaks or even full-length presentations. Use several individuals who best meet the needs of various age groups, children through adults.

(These stories may also be used when another program you produce does not completely fill the allocated time slot.)

(51) The Bible Speaks—Encourage people to call in or write to you about what the Bible has to say on certain topics of concern to them. Offer clear, concise answers on this program. Using several program personalities to answer questions will improve flow and variety.

(52) Today's Christian—Contemporary issues which impact the Christian life are discussed and suggestions made for a proper Christian response.

(53) Living Archives—Incidents in the history of your church (or all area churches) are shared with viewers. The incidents may be humorous, serious, trend setting, and so forth. These factual stories are one way of sharing the pilgrimage of the local church (or churches) in the quest to reach and serve the local community. Such vignettes can be in the form of spot announcements, miniprograms, or even entire programs if ample information is available. Church volunteers will gladly look up this information for you. They will be pleased to know that church history is being emphasized on television.

(54) Inside Church Architecture—This program features the unique architecture of local church buildings. Include an explanation of the type of architecture as well as noteworthy features of the local structure. Explain why this particular design was chosen for the church.

Also, feature interiors. If there are unusual furnishings or decorations, cover these. For instance, one church did an entire program on the cross-stitched wall hangings and their significance to church history.

(55) The Family Friend—One major concern to today's family is covered in each program. The pastor may host the program, along with appropriate resource persons for certain topics. Viewers are encouraged to send in suggestions for future programs. Topics may be restricted to spiritual help or cover the broad range of concern for strengthening families.

(56) A Pastor's Perspective—This program is a televised pastor's conference similar in some ways to suggestion number 13 for music directors. One local pastor shares his ongoing perspective on ministry with other ministers. Or, hosting the program can be delegated among pastors. Tapes may even be exchanged with distant areas where a similar program is produced for cablecasting.

(57) Welcome Minister—New pastors and other ministers are introduced to the community via cable. Using an interview format, viewers learn about the minister's background, training, family, hobbies, and other items of human interest.

(58) Meet the Minister—This idea starter is similar to number 57, but is a weekly or monthly feature. The purpose is to introduce each local minister, not just new ones.

(59) Welcome, Neighbor!—Newcomers to the community often must find out important information in "bits and pieces." As a service to the community and as a way of introducing your

church, produce a program highlighting the community and important local information (emergency telephone numbers, where to secure utility hookups, etc.). Periodically show the program on cable. Local town officials and the cable company will embrace the idea.

(60) Pastor- (or Minister)-of-the-Week—A different pastor each week is given the opportunity of delivering a devotional thought for the community. If your church does the program alone, you may feature other staff ministers on a rotating basis.

(61) Layperson to Layperson—Similar to idea number 60, a different layperson from your church is featured each week. This person shares a personal testimony and/or devotional thought as one layperson to another.

(62) Community Calendar—During one of your programs or at a programming break, provide a calendar of upcoming local events. You provide a valuable service and foster goodwill.

(63) Bible Facts—This is a religious game show, pitting individuals or panels against each other. Contestants may be drawn from within the church or several churches. The latter suggestion heightens enthusiasm and broadens the audience potential.

(64) Coffee with the Pastor—This is a regular devotional program hosted by the pastor. Its name suggests an early morning time slot.

(65) Ask the Mayor—As a community service, allocate a portion of one of your programs for a write-in or call-in segment which features the town's mayor. If people feel they can gain answers to their questions, they will be in your audience at air time. Consider using other local officials, too.

(66) Bible Journey—Read Scripture, preferably with words appearing on the screen. Also, you may wish to include slides from a Bible scene set. Use a regular pattern of Scripture reading so that all major portions of the Bible are referenced in the course of a year. Choose a reader who has a pleasant reading voice and exercises care to properly pronounce words.

(67) Scriptural Interlude—Superimpose and "roll" Scripture passages over local scenes with musical accompaniment as a spot announcement or mini-program.

[Note: Be certain that the music you use is cleared for broadcast.]

(68) Christian Talent Time—Plan a series of programs which feature members of the church with various talents: singing, dramatic monologues, and so on. Carefully evaluate effect of each individual upon the audience. Some of these people may have the potential for hosting their own future productions.

(69) Help Wanted—This series of programs highlights local sources of aid for various problems. Of course, you will want to present your church as a source of help for spiritual and other needs.

Inform your viewers where they may find emergency housing, shelter for abused wives and children, clothing, and so on.

(70) Partners with Youth—Consider a series of programs on local youth-serving agencies which seek to meet the needs of youth in partnership with the church. Three of these agencies with such a stated objective are: Boy Scouts of America, Girl Scouts of the United States of America, and Camp Fire. There are, perhaps, numerous others in your community.

(71) Christian Homemaker—With so many women working outside the home, pressure mounts regarding use of available time. This program offers tips on housecleaning, maintaining a devotional life, getting proper exercise, and other pertinent topics. Interview a different Christian homemaker on each show.

(72) Special Feature Series—Allocate time and funding for televising of periodic special features such as an Easter drama and musical, a Christmas special, children's choir concerts, and others. Invest required planning time to make these special events worth repeating. Subsequent productions will be eagerly anticipated by viewers and more easily planned by producers.

(73) Community Special Events—Increase community support and meet community needs by cablecasting happenings like the town's annual Christmas parade. Do not worry about carrying the event "live." Taped is better since you will

have all of the parade participants, their families and friends as additional viewers.

(74) Video Newsletter—If you have unlimited access to cable time, one innovative idea for church members is a periodic video newsletter rather than a mail out. When this program is produced well, prospective members will also enjoy viewing the cable presentation. Therefore, a video newsletter becomes an outreach opportunity.

(75) Tax Tips—There will always be a need for tax preparation help. Since so much attention is often focused on federal taxes, maybe help on state taxes would be welcomed by your community. This program utilizes some of your lay people.

Appendix C:
One Hundred Uses of Video in Religious Education and Church Programming

Once the church has access to a videocassette recorder or player and a television set, you are ready to begin using video in religious education and church programming. Addition of an inexpensive camera further broadens the opportunities.

Some of the suggestions given below are for in-house productions. However, hundreds of prerecorded tapes are available: (1) on a free-loan basis, (2) via satellite-delivered subscription services, and (3) from videotape rental outlets. (See the source directory for details. Also, see "Seventy-Five Programming Ideas for Local Cable/LPTV Productions" for suggestions on the other facets of video usage by the church.)

Be creative in your uses of video. The following are merely idea starters:

Religious Education

1. *Special Guests*—Record guest teachers and speakers at your church for later use. Identify, store, and circulate these tapes through the church media library (church library).

[Note: Ask permission before recording a speaker. Some speakers have contracts which prohibit this practice.]

2. *Teaching Methods*—Record Sunday School teachers employing a variety of teaching methods. Use the tapes for personal evaluation.

3. *Leadership Training*—Secure professionally produced leadership training tapes which demonstrate proper methods, techniques, preparation practices, and so on. Use the tapes in ongoing worker planning meetings.

4. *Children's Curriculum Support*—Record or use a prerecorded tape for inclusion in interest centers for Children's Sunday School departments. Even if the interest-center approach is not used in your curriculum, these attention getters will enhance the lesson.

5. *Pastoral Comments*—When the pastor is unable to be in a class but wishes to make a contribution, record his comments on videotape.

6. *Discussion*—Videotape actual local happenings in your community; borrow a tape from a church member or library, or record from television situations which pertain to the teaching objectives. Showing these portrayals will often be the "sparks" that "ignite" a productive class discussion.

7. *Absentee Training*—Tape in-house leadership training events and planning sessions for those unable to be present and for others enlisted to serve after the "live" event.

8. *Point of View*—To orient workers in preschool and children's departments, record some scenes as the child would see them. This will help workers remember to mount pictures lower on the wall, hold teaching aids at the proper eye level, and so forth.

9. *Demonstration*—Some lessons are learned better by seeing them demonstrated properly. For instance, tape someone operating several pieces of audiovisual equipment or correctly holding a hymnal. Pupils will learn faster than merely hearing a verbal explanation. And you will not be required to bring all of the items into a small classroom.

10. *Interpersonal Reactions*—Record actual meetings such as Sunday School classes and training groups. Be careful to capture reactions, group functions, and nonverbal communication.

Use this tape with workers so they may evaluate their leadership styles and responses of groups to these styles.

11. Vacation Bible School—Record highlights of your Vacation Bible School. Show excerpts of the tape at VBS Parents' Night. Review the entire tape with your planning group as you evaluate the current Bible School and project for next year.

12. Comparative Religion—Record worship services of other faiths for use in training groups studying various religions.

13. Special Training Applications—Prepare training tapes for groups such as ushers, greeters, and deacons. These tapes will better portray content than a purchased tape since they feature your surroundings and your particular approaches.

14. Poor Technique Demonstration—Videotape a demonstration group utilizing poor teaching techniques. Use this tape in leadership training sessions. (A demonstration group is suggested rather than an actual group to avoid unnecessary embarrassment of workers. They *will* get the point without creating an unfortunate situation.)

15. Follow-up—Prepare a follow-up, reinforcement tape for in-church training events. Make video equipment available for individual study, too. Also, check out tapes for in-home viewing where possible.

16. Continuing Education—Use tapes to update leaders on new teaching methods, new resources, new developments, and other continuing education experiences.

17. Ongoing Worker Meetings—Employ videotapes for curriculum reviews and teacher preparation in weekly workers' meetings. Several suppliers produce videotapes for these weekly meetings. Also, satellite-delivered services such as Baptist Telecommunication Network (BTN) provide materials for multiple curriculum lines, including one based on the International Sunday School lessons.

18. Conference Sharing—Get in the habit of taking a videocassette recorder and camera to out-of-town conferences. Bring back the tape to share with co-workers.

19. Sunday School on Wheels—Record Sunday School classes. Take the tape, along with a portable video player, curriculum piece, and get-well card to a sick member.

[Note: Several manufacturers now produce inexpensive video players which connect easily to an ordinary television set.]

20. Small-Group Study—Assemble a basic religious education collection of videocassettes in the church media library (church library) for checkout to Bible study groups.

21. Rotating Collection—Regularly borrow or rent videocassettes which support Bible study and training curriculum pieces. Make these tapes available through a "branch" library set up in the weekly workers' meeting area.

22. In-Home Religious Education—Design an in-home religious education program using videotape. (Many American homes have or soon will have video playback capability.)

23. Central Control "Feed"—Wire classrooms for closed-circuit television and originate programming from a central area such as the office or library. This relatively inexpensive procedure gives you great flexibility for making targeted presentations within a brief time span.

Several churches have been using this technique for a number of years. Some even have the capability of simultaneously distributing multiple video programs within the church plant. (As you plan new educational space, include the "stringing" of coaxial cable to all rooms. When you are ready to initiate the system, cables will be in place, and you will have far less expense.)

24. Multilingual—Use the second audio track available on some videorecorders to place another language on existing videotape. This second track can be used in the religious education program with language groups and for English classes for those who do not fluently speak the language. (Use of this second track does not disturb the existing English track.)

25. Multiplied Effectiveness—Use an outstanding Bible storyteller to record a series of stories for children. This approach shares the talents of individuals with many people in a way far beyond what they could do in person.

26. Interactive Tape—Prepare a videotape

which requires the learner to get the correct answer before proceeding with a lesson. If you do not have a videocassette recorder with interactive capabilities, you can still make a tape to use in conjunction with a curriculum piece.

27. Interactive Discs—A number of laser videodiscs are now available, especially if your church operates a school. Some simple programs may be used with only a laser videodisc player. Others require connection to a personal computer.

28. Prepared Computer Programs—Religious education programs are available for most personal computers. Many of these programs are Bible knowledge games. (See appendix H for software and hardware listings, and for computer organizations whose members prepare and distribute a variety of religious education materials.)

29. Do-It-Yourself Computer Programs—Tailor-make your own programs for use in religious education. A growing number of ministers and lay people are pursuing such projects as hobbies.

Worship

30. Worship Education—Teach children and adults the basic facets and forms of public and private worship via critiques of actual taped worship services.

31. Staff Evaluation—Record the worship services for a weekly evaluation by the pastor, church staff, and others involved in worship leadership.

32. Seasonal Programs—Record special seasonal programs for use in later years, for planning other worship services, and for possible cablecasting/broadcasting.

33. Sermon Delivery—Pastors can study their delivery techniques by viewing tapes made of the worship services.

New Church Member Orientation

34. In-Home Visits—Make a videotape to take into the homes of new members, introducing them to the church staff, programming, and ministries.

35. Training—Tape new church member orientation sessions for in-church and in-home use as well as for possible cablecasting to members of other churches of like faith. These sessions include distinctives of the faith and unique features of the local church. They may serve as the actual orientation sessions or as a reinforcement. (A better use of video is for the tapes to serve as reinforcement rather than the actual orientation sessions.)

36. Tour—A videotaped tour of the church plant is helpful to new members, especially if the church is large. You may find many other members wishing to see the tape.

Member Enrichment

37. Information—Prepare a program on what the church is seeking to accomplish in the next year or so. Use the tape in a general assembly. Take the tape to homes of those not present in the assembly.

38. Every-Member Canvass—Include a brief videotaped presentation in the homes as you conduct an every-member developmental or stewardship canvass. Rather than simply coming to retrieve a form or pledge card, the canvasser helps individuals and families feel more involved in the church family. (See the "stewardship" section for more suggestions.)

39. Staff Perspective—Interview church staff members in informal settings, getting their observations on the church program and potential. This is particularly meaningful to homebound individuals who may have no other opportunity to interact with some of these persons. Another interesting approach would be to interview church members on the same topics for sharing with homebound individuals.

Outreach/Ministry

40. Homebound—Take videotapes of worship services and special events to homebound church members and prospects.

41. Nursing Home Ministries—Prepare special videotaped programs as well as recordings of regular worship services and other events to share at nursing homes in assemblies or by closed-circuit television to all rooms.

42. Hospital Ministry—Produce special videotapes for play over hospital closed-circuit systems.

Enlist the help of the hospital chaplain in determining content to meet the needs of the broadest target audience.

43. Fair Promotion—Prepare a church promotional tape for continuous play in a booth or display during a public event like a county fair. Keep the content people oriented, showing various age groups involved in fellowship and learning experiences. You may wish to have more than one tape available to respond to specific inquiries. [Do not leave the tape to do the work. Have several members present for interaction with inquirers.]

44. Prospect Outreach—Use free-loan tapes of special interest to identifiable prospect groups as a program feature for an outreach fellowship. Some examples are: sporting events, hunting and fishing shows, travel tapes, craft demonstrations, and cooking shows.

45. Promotion/Planning—Record highlights of the church recreation program for showing in a churchwide fellowship period. This will stimulate interest. Use the tape also in planning and critiquing recreational ministries.

46. School Athletics—Record highlights of a school sporting event to show at an after-game fellowship.

47. Outings—Take a videocassette recorder on a church outing. At a later date, play the tape to show others how beneficial the experience was for the participants. Or, use the tape for a follow-up fellowship for participants.

Stewardship

48. Budget Preparation—In addition to the earlier suggestion of an every-member canvass, prepare a brief tape on church ministries and activities to educate the budget planning committee prior to accepting allocation requests and the actual structuring of the upcoming budget.

49. Budget Requests—Instead of suggestion number 48, help everyone asking for sizable increases or for major segments of the budget to prepare a tape illustrating some of the benefits which will be realized from this expenditure. Show actual happenings during the current year and project benefits for the next year.

50. Budget Promotion—Prepare a tape similar to the one suggested in number 48. Use it in a churchwide promotional event prior to budget vote and subscription. This may be presented in a worship service or in a special assembly during Bible study hour.

51. Stewardship Education—Show a prerecorded tape each month which demonstrates the work of some agency or mission board which receives support through your budget. Prepare your own tape to illustrate local denominational or church involvement.

52. Motivation—Rent stewardship motivational tapes for showing during the annual stewardship emphasis or for periodic emphases throughout the year.

Youth Ministry

53. Parent-Youth Dialogues—Interview young people and parents expressing views on roles of parents or teenagers. Use the tapes as dialogue starters for a parent-teen session or youth training event.

54. Ethical Role Playing—Let the young people do role playing on tape for later critique and teaching sessions. Some ideas are: (1) peer pressure to do something wrong, (2) being judgmental of others, and (3) cheating on a test.

55. Vocational Guidance—Interest youth in Christian vocations by showing tapes of actual individuals sharing about their work. Some of these tapes are available from free loan or rental libraries. But why not prepare some of these tapes locally?

56. Fellowship—Rent tapes of movies for fellowships. Hundreds of titles are available for your use.

[Note: If tapes are secured locally rather than through a tape library, ask someone at the rental firm if the program has been cleared for public viewing, not simply for an in-home showing.]

57. Attendance Emphasis—Prepare videotapes of members and prospects which will be shown at a future event. People on the tape will be certain to attend the event, thus building attendance.

58. *Youth Rallies*—Bring outstanding youth speakers and singing groups to youth rallies via videotape or even via satellite!

Church Administration

59. *Orientation*—Tape orientation sessions for use with all church staff members. Each new worker hears and sees exactly the same thing as everyone else regarding procedures, work schedules, safety considerations, fringe benefits, and other important matters.

60. *Staff Enrichment*—Regularly update church staff members on denominational developments, new programs, methods, and professional development opportunities.

61. *Maintenance Program Help*—Borrow tapes from equipment manufacturers or distributors for instructing maintenance personnel on the proper use and care of equipment and products.

62. *Committee Training*—Prepare a tape which explains basic procedures for committees: meeting times, making budget requests, securing church approval of proposals, calendaring procedures, and so forth.

Christian Life in Action

63. *Expressions of Concern*—Make a tape on concerns of your church members or the entire Christian community for sharing with local civic leaders in city council meetings or in other public forums. Visualization will strengthen your request for action.

64. *Local Response to Need*—Prepare a program on local needs—poverty, poor housing, unemployment, and so forth—and offer solutions which your members can make possible with their actions.

65. *Hunger*—Secure prerecorded tapes on world hunger for use during a food drive or world hunger offering. You may wish to use brief segments of a tape in a series of worship series.

Marriage and Family

66. *Counseling*—Use a recorder and camera in marriage counseling sessions to reveal verbal and nonverbal communication between spouses.

67. *Marital Education*—Purchase a series of premarital education tapes which are to be viewed by couples prior to being married in your church.

68. *Family Night at the Movies*—Rent videotapes (entertaining or "mildly educational") for use in periodic family night activities at church. These tapes may serve as the catalyst to draw families together for fellowship.

69. *Family Night at Home*—Secure some tapes which can be checked out of the church media library for viewing in the home. Also, check out videocassette recorders or videoplayers to families who do not own them. The purpose of this service is to encourage individual families to have at-home nights together. Provide other suggested activities to supplement the tapes. (In addition to purchasing entertainment features, make available recorded church activities like musicals, dramas, mission trip highlights, and other programs featuring church members.)

70. *Model Weddings*—Tape a model wedding and/or rehearsal to show families during planning and preparation for an upcoming wedding. Also include on the tape any church-adopted policies, procedures, and costs. By using this approach, everyone gets the same information.

71. *Wedding Gifts*—Videotape actual weddings in your church and give the tapes to participants on a cost-recovery basis. (Maybe a wedding fee could cover this cost without asking for additional funds.)

72. *Baptisms*—Similar to number 71, record baptisms and offer the tapes to the families on a cost-recovery basis.

73. *Fiftieth Anniversaries*—Tape highlights of in-church fiftieth wedding anniversaries or receptions. Offer the tapes for cost recovery.

Special Applications

74. *Ministerial Tributes*—Tape highlights of an individual minister's ongoing ministry as a tribute during a significant anniversary observance, retirement occasion, or a going-away fellowship.

75. *Staff Appreciations*—Similar to number

74, honor any longtime staff member, including secretarial staff, child-care staff, maintenance staff, and so on.

76. *Staff Welcome*—Give a new church staff member a warm welcome and preserve the event by giving a tape of the welcome fellowship.

77. *Church Waiting Area Feature*—For individuals waiting in the church office, play a videotape introducing new church programs, ministries, and upcoming events. This will be informative to members and may interest prospective members. (After all, any person not a member of another local church is a prospect!)

78. *Public Waiting Area*—Play videotaped religious dramas, biblical reenactments, devotional thoughts, and other church productions in public areas such as doctors' and dentists' offices, hospital waiting rooms, and so forth. Include an appropriate "commercial" for your church.

Missions

79. *Tour Highlights*—Record highlights from church mission tours and share them with the church family. Participation and funding of future tours are sure to increase.

80. *Missionary Reports*—Play prerecorded tapes provided by your denomination of missionaries giving on-the-field reports. These tapes are especially useful for missions organization meetings as well as special offering and churchwide missions emphases. Such tapes are already available for loan as well as via satellite.

81. *Missions Teleconferences*—Encourage your church to participate in a missions teleconference, either "live" or by tape. Several denominations are making this possible. The programs feature missions reports, followed by a period of call-in questions.

82. *Personal Missions Report*—Provide a missionary with a portable videocassette recorder and camera with which he can send your church a videotaped newsletter.

83. *Video Care Cassette*—Make and send periodic tapes to a missionary family or several missionary families who have compatible video equipment. These tapes will help them keep abreast of what is happening back home and will show the missionaries you are remembering them.

84. *Missionary Family Support*—Periodically purchase a family-oriented movie and send it to a missionary family on the field.

Music Ministry

85. *Specials*—Tape your special programs for later viewing in the library or even for cablecasting/broadcasting.

[Note: be certain to secure appropriate permission from the copyright holders for certain types of tapes and distributions.]

86. *Tape Exchange*—Exchange tapes with other church music ministries to study techniques and gain new ideas for your church. Also, you may be able to critique others and correct problems in your own choir without confrontation.

87. *Performance Evaluation*—Videotape choir rehearsals prior to public performances for evaluation. Make suggestions for improvement. Encourage discussion by choir members.

88. *Choir Appearance Critique*—Tape the choir as they listen to the minister deliver his sermon on television. Perhaps some habits need to be broken, and these will become evident when viewing the tape.

89. *Music Minister Evaluation*—Videotape the minister of music to allow for him to evaluate leadership and directing styles, pacing of the service and projected personality.

90. *Accompanist Evaluation*—Similar to number 89, tape the accompanists for their evaluation of style and appearance.

Historical Preservation

91. *Building Archives*—Record all major church events for safekeeping in the church archives.

92. *First-Person History*—Record older members recalling church history from the first-person viewpoint. (In audiotaping, this is called "oral history.") No written document can capture the mood and expression of the videotape.

93. *Historical Emphasis*—To underscore the importance of preserving church history and to

educate new members, show selected videotapes of historical church events. You may even want to calendar an annual historical observance.

94. Architectural Perspective—Interview the architects who designed your buildings, asking them why certain styles and features were included in the construction. This will be informative to later church history "buffs."

Evangelism

95. Testimonies for Witnessing—Tape dynamic personal testimonies and use them in witnessing encounters, including in-home visits.

96. Training—Make a training tape which demonstrates how to make a faith-sharing visit.

97. Witness Motivation—Prepare a witnessing motivation tape of individuals who become Christians because of others sharing their faith. Close each testimony with, "What if you had not come?"

Multichurch Involvements

98. Unique Ministries—Prepare a tape on unique ministries of the churches in a certain locale, area, or state and share it with other churches. Highlight positive differences among churches. A tape exchange network may even be formed by interested churches. Also, share a copy of the tape with regional denominational offices for historical and promotional purposes.

99. Shared Concerns—Prepare a report to denominational leadership, expressing viewpoints or concerns of the congregation regarding current denominational issues.

100. Shared Ministries—Record shared projects of the churches in an area. Use the tape to gain further interest by other churches, to broaden community support, and to report to sponsoring churches.

Appendix D:
Checklist for Using Videotape in Religious Education

When using videotape, you should be certain that:

____ You know how to properly operate the video recorder/player to be used.

____ The recorder/player is clean and in good condition.

____ The tape is the correct width and format (2", 1", ½" VHS, ½" Beta, ¼", 8mm).

____ The tape is threaded correctly, if an open-reel format is used.

____ When recording, the script is carefully planned, written, and rehearsed.

____ Content of the tape is suited to the needs of the viewer.

____ The screen of the monitor is large enough to be seen by everyone, or multiple monitors are used.

____ Tapes, recorder/player and television/monitor are reserved in the church media library well in advance.

____ Appropriate cables and connectors are reserved, also.

____ Tapes are previewed.

____ Adequate introduction and follow-up are used.

____ Only meaningful portions of the tape are used.

____ The equipment is operating properly before the audience arrives.

____ Sound levels are checked before and after the audience arrives.

If you are troubleshooting a video recorder:

____ Check the power switch on the machine.

____ Check all connections between the recorder and power source (use a continuity tester/check visually/wiggle the cord/looks for cracks and frays); between the recorder and monitor/receiver (television); between the recorder and camera; between the recorder and microphone.

____ Check to see that there is power in the receptacle. (Use a neon tester or plug in a piece of equipment known to work.)

____ Check switches to see that they are set on the proper functions.

____ Check all controls for proper levels.

____ Check for bad tape by using a tape known to be good.

____ Inspect heads for evidence of dirt.

- *Remember: safety first!*

____ Do not check exposed electrical components with the unit connected to electricity.

____ Do not "tinker" with the equipment beyond your level of training and understanding.

____ If you are unsuccessful after basic troubleshooting procedures have been employed, take the unit to an authorized service center.

Appendix E:
Video Equipment Maintenance Suggestions

Simple, preventive maintenance procedures on video equipment can save your church sizable repair costs in the future. Beyond these easy-to-do maintenance procedures, however, leave the more complex repairs to professionals.

Some General Suggestions—Three rules apply to maintaining any type of video equipment:

First, store hardware and software in a clean, dry place. Two of the greatest enemies of video equipment are dust and moisture. Particles of dust settling into a machine or the case of a videocassette, videodisc, or computer disk are like small pieces of sandpaper being placed there. Moisture corrodes connectors and generally renders a piece of equipment inoperable. In addition to storing hardware and software in as dry an environment as possible, never place containers with liquids on top of a piece of equipment. One cup of spilled coffee can cost you hundreds—even thousands—of dollars.

Second, maintain a comfortable temperature in the storage area. Heat extremes are harmful and, to some extent, so are cold extremes. If you are comfortable, temperature is probably acceptable.

Third, when doing any kind of maintenance, disconnect the power source. Do *not* take needless chances. You could encounter a live contact.

Videocassette Recorders—After every one hundred hours of operation, your VCR needs a thorough cleaning. Supplies for the task are: cellular swabs, VCR head cleaning solution, a static-free cloth, a head demagnetizer, and a can of compressed air (specifically designed for cleaning photo and video equipment). Follow these steps:

(1) *Remove the cover of the recorder.* This procedure usually requires loosening a few screws on the cabinet.

(2) *Blow away any loose dust particles with the compressed air.* This is particularly useful in areas you will not be able to reach with the cleaning swabs. Do not place the air nozzle close to delicate parts. The force of air will be sufficient at some distance.

(3) *Gently clean the video heads with a cellular foam swab (not cotton) and a head-cleaning solution.* Use only side-to-side or horizontal motion on these delicate heads located on the shiny steel drum. The number of heads on a machine will vary from model to model. Choose a solution made specifically for cleaning videoheads or 90 percent isopropyl alcohol. (A 90 percent solution of isopropyl alcohol may be found at any drugstore. Do not use regular isopropyl alcohol which has a higher water content and can cause corrosion.)

(4) *Clean the other heads on the recorder, too.* These include the control track, audio, and erase heads. Use the same cleaning solution and a horizontal motion.

(5) *Next, thoroughly clean the tape path: rollers, guides, and other parts which may come in contact with the tape.*

[Note: There are a number of video cleaning cassettes available today. Frequent use of these cassettes (as directed) will keep your VCR much cleaner, but they cannot reach some of the areas you can with the cleaning swab. If you decide to use a cleaning cassette as a supplementary tool, choose one which incorporates a liquid in the process. These are known as "wet" cleaners. Using a "dry" cleaner is not recommended since many of them have an abrasive action which can damage video heads. Replacing the heads often costs nearly half as much as the original VCR purchase

Appendix E: Video Equipment Maintenance Suggestions

price, so you do not want to damage the heads!]

(6) *Demagnetize the heads.* Using an inexpensive head demagnetizer (found at many electronics stores) will remove any magnetism which has occurred during regular operation. Magnetism will damage tapes and cause the VCR to play improperly. The demagnetizing procedure is accomplished by: (1) turning on the demagnetizer while several inches from the head, (2) bringing the tool to *almost* touching the head, (3) moving the demagnetizer's tip around the head surface (without touching it), (4) withdrawing the tool several inches from the head, and (5) turning it off. Repeat this procedure for all video, erase, and control track heads.

(7) *Replace the VCR cover and tighten screws.*

(8) *Wipe the case/cabinet with an antistatic cloth.*

(9) *Protect the unit with its original cover or a piece of plastic or fabric.* Do not turn the machine on when the cover is in place. A heat buildup will seriously damage equipment. [Note: Exercise care with your videotapes, too. They must be stored vertically in a clean, comfortable environment. To avoid accidental erasure, do not store tapes near large electric motors or other high-energy sources. Do not attempt to splice tapes. The glue used for splicing may damage the heads. Moreover, the spliced segment will cause a picture "breakup" on each playback. Protect your tape investment. It can become sizable.]

Video Cameras—Cameras allow for little user maintenance. You can take these maintenance and preventive measures:

(1) *Blow away dust particles from the camera lens with a can of compressed air.*

(2) *Gently clean the lens with lintless lens tissues and lens cleaner available at a video or photography store.*

(3) *Wipe off the case with an antistatic cloth.*

(4) *Avoid carrying the camera lens pointed straight down.* This can damage the pickup tube(s).

(5) *Never point the camera lens toward a bright light source such as the sun or a video light.* Such an action may burn this image permanently into the pickup tube. Often, the burned tube is irreparable. [Sometimes the camera can be focused onto an illuminated white surface with increasing exposure times to, in essence, burn the entire tube. This procedure may diminish the impact of the single burned spot. In cases where this effort is successful, tube effectiveness and life span are still reduced significantly.]

(6) *Turn the camera on regularly, even if you do not plan to use it.* Unused cameras age very quickly.

Television Receivers/Monitors—You are most familiar with this video component. There is probably at least one television set in your home. Follow these suggestions in addition to the general ones made in the beginning of this appendix item:

(1) *Clean the screen frequently with a lintless cloth moistened with a glass-cleaning solution.*

(2) *Wipe the cabinet with an antistatic cloth.*

(3) *Do not attempt to service internal parts.* Televisions store sizable charges of electricity long after a set has been turned off. Serious electrical shock can occur when an untrained individual "tinkers" in the cabinet.

Laser Videodisc Players—The general suggestions already mentioned for equipment maintenance are most of the preventive steps possible for a videodisc player. It is particularly important to keep dust particles away from the discs. Store discs vertically in a cool place. Also, wipe the player frequently with an antistatic cloth.

Personal Computers—Dirt and static electricity are two key enemies of computers. In addition to general suggestions above, perform the following maintenance and take these preventive actions:

(1) *Keep the computer away from smoke, other air contaminants, grease, and so on.*

(2) *Take off your computer covers at least twice a year and remove internal dirt.* (Some computers are sealed and will not allow entry by a consumer.) Use the compressed air referred to earlier, along with tweezers, to remove accumulations of dust. [Note: Wait approximately thirty minutes after unplugging the computer prior to entry. This will avoid exposure to stored electrical energy in the computer.]

(3) *Replace the cover and wipe the computer case with an antistatic cloth.*

(4) *Clean the printer, removing ink buildup, ribbon fibers, and paper scraps.* Frequency for this procedure will be determined by the amount of printer use.

(5) *Clean the disk drive with one of the commercially available head-cleaning diskettes.*

(6) *Clean the data cassette player with a head-cleaning cassette (liquid type) or with swabs and 90 percent isopropyl alcohol (except rubber parts).*

(7) *Demagnetize all recording heads in the cassette player and disk drive, using the same procedure as described for videocassette recorders.*

(8) *Keep sources of magnetic energy away from hardware and software.* A few of the sources are telephones; speakers; electrical devices such as radios, televisions, calculators, typewriters, and magnetized tools like scissors and screwdrivers.

(9) *Keep clutter away from the computer to allow for free circulation of air.* Some computers generate sizable amounts of heat that, if contained within the unit, will damage sensitive parts.

(10) *Avoid static electricity which severely damages hardware and software.* Two sources of static electricity are shuffling feet and low humidity. Preventive measures include using: three-prong plugs and electric outlets to provide grounding, antistatic floor mats, humidifiers to raise the relative humidity, antistatic products for the floor, and antistatic cloths for wiping the video screen.

(11) *Protect the system from power spikes with a surge protector.* An alternate power supply is also wise in areas subject to frequent power problems.

Other Video Equipment—Most other video equipment requires trained service technicians, yet some preventive maintenance steps are offered in the instruction manuals. Follow the suggested procedures, maintain a clean, relatively dry environment and insist on a comfortable temperature range. These guidelines will minimize your repair costs.

Note: Attempting to repair your equipment during warranty period will negate the equipment's warranty.

Appendix F:
Video Production Hints

The purpose of this section is not to tell you everything about producing a video program. The material will, however, give you an introduction to the subject if you are searching for a brief overview which will help as you guide volunteers or other staff members involved in production; read on!

First, recognize the limitations of personnel and equipment. Producing a videotape for use as a Vacation Bible School Parent's Night feature, recording a worship service to take to the home of a shut-in, or recording a Bible study for cable television may be where more church leaders now find themselves than producing a gala television special which "rivals the networks." If these simpler programs meet the felt needs for which they were produced, they are just as important or maybe more important than the gala special.

Keep in mind these observations if you are considering video production or have begun the process:

(1) There is a direct parallel between the experience, skill, and equipment used by a producer and the quality of the final product.

(2) Inexpensive equipment in the hands of beginners will not yield "Hollywood" quality. Do not have unrealistic expectations for such a production. And do not worry if every training tape does not meet the network standards of excellence.

(3) As experience in planning skills increase, along with the natural flow of creativity, quality will rise to the capabilities of your equipment. Some excellent training tapes and cable television productions have been done on low budgets by sensitive, caring people with little or no video training.

Second, become familiar with key production personnel titles and responsibilities. Small-scale productions do not require a person for each of the titles listed below. As few as two or three volunteers may be the entire production. However, every major *function* must be addressed if the production is planned properly:

Producer—the person ultimately responsible for the program or series of programs, its design, scheduling, quality, content, financing, and distribution. In many churches, the pastor is the producer.

Director—the person who transforms the script into reality. He has usually had experience with video equipment. He also has skills in working with people, a sense of mood and pacing, an ability to draw out the abilities/personalities of on-camera personalities, an understanding of lighting and composition, an eye for what "looks good," and an ear for what "sounds good." Once the production is in progress, the director literally and figuratively "calls the shots."

[If you do not have a person in your church who meets all of these criteria, look for someone who has the required innate abilities. Introduce that person to the production process and provide exposure to training as it becomes available.

Camera Persons—the persons who are responsible for obtaining camera shots called for by the director. Given the simplicity of most cameras today, camera operators can be trained rather easily. Look for persons who exhibit a sense of caring about their work, give attention to details, and follow directions well. An understanding of shot composition, camera movements, and overall camera operation will come with experience.

Engineer/Technician—the person responsible for adjusting and keeping the equipment in proper order. Though an engineer is certainly preferable, this is not required for church productions. Someone, however, must ultimately be responsible for the equipment. This person knows his limitations and is willing to secure outside help when necessary.

Since much of today's equipment is relatively easy to operate, there may be a temptation to let everyone handle his own equipment's adjustments. Do not allow this to happen. Someone must be in charge of making the entire system work as a unit.

Writers—persons who write well and have been taught television techniques. These persons do not require a television background. However, they must receive at least minimal orientation to television production, so they will know how to maximize video's strengths and avoid its limitations. Also, they must be able to write for a visual medium. Television is a far more visual media form than an audio one. Often, a few well-chosen words are better than a lengthy discourse.

Technical Director—the person who works under supervision of the director to actually do the switching between cameras, monitor audio levels and, perhaps, make minor adjustments on the camera control units. If a technical director is used, the director is free to follow the script more closely.

Floor Manager—a person responsible for appearance of the program's set and availability of props. During the actual shooting, the floor manager wears headphones like the camera operators. She cares for arrangements on the set, including cueing on-camera personalities related to pacing, time remaining, and upcoming camera changes.

As the key leader, you should be able to give at least the basic cues used by a floor manager to on-camera talent:

(1) "You are on this camera"—finger pointed toward camera lens.

(2) "Slow down, relax"—palms of both hand turned downward, held at about waist level in front of you.

(3) "Watch your time"—finger pointed toward wristwatch.

(4) "Everything is fine—OK"—tips of thumb and forefinger held together with three remaining fingers pointing upward.

(5) "Three minutes left"—three middle fingers pointed upward.

(6) "Go faster"—two hands in a forward-rolling motion, one hand passing over the other.

(7) "One minute left"—forefinger uplifted.

(8) "Fifteen seconds left"—clenched fist with knuckles pointed upward and palm turned toward on-camera talent.

(9) "Cut/stop"—hand drawn across throat as if in a cutting motion.

Other Functions—Persons holding positions previously mentioned or other individuals working under their supervision will need to be assigned these tasks:

(1) recording the audio portion of a program, including responsibility for microphones and their placement;

(2) operating the film chain, if used (see glossary);

(3) editing the tape;

(4) lighting the set or sets;

(5) designing and constructing the set or sets;

(6) securing all needed props;

(7) arranging for any music to be used in the production;

(8) creating graphics, both nonprojecteds (posters, charts, and so forth) and projecteds (slides, overhead transparencies, and so forth);

(9) applying makeup, when needed.

Third, be familiar with basic camera directions. Everyone involved in a production will benefit from learning and using proper camera directions. This is true whether you have a crew of one or twenty. These directions remove ambiguity and enable the camera operator to move the camera in a proper direction each time:

(1) Pan—the direction given for horizontally turning a camera to the left or right. To "pan left" means to turn the camera from the right edge of a scene to the left edge of a scene (as seen by the camera operator). In other words, move horizontally toward the direction indicated by the director. To "pan right" would be to move from left to right horizontally.

(2) Tilt—to pivot the camera up or down on a

Appendix F: Video Production Hints

tripod head. "Up" and "down" are based on the direction which the camera lens moves. "Tilt down" means to maneuver the camera so that the lens moves toward the floor. "Tilt up" means to maneuver the camera so that the lens moves away from the floor.

(3) Dolly—to roll the entire camera (on its dolly) toward the subject ("dolly in") or away from the subject ("dolly out").

(4) Zoom—to adjust the camera's zoom lens from a wide shot to a telephoto/close-up ("zoom in") or from a telephoto/close-up to a wide shot ("zoom out").

(5) Truck—to roll the entire camera (on its dolly) laterally or side to side. "Truck left" means to roll the camera to the operator's left toward the left side of a scene, and "truck right" means to roll the camera to the operator's right toward the right side of a scene.

(6) Hold—the directive for keeping a camera in the same position.

Along with camera directions, the types of shots being requested of a camera operator have standardized terminology, too:

(1) High Angle—to elevate the camera so the subject is below the camera level.

(2) Low Angle—to lower the camera so the subject is above the camera level.

(3) Long Shot—a very wide picture. In a studio setting, most, if not all, of the set would be revealed in a long shot.

(4) Medium Shot—an intermediate-sized picture. In a studio setting, the shot might include all of a person and the immediate surroundings.

(5) Close-Up—a picture in which the subject fills most of the screen. If a close-up shot of a person is called for, this will usually mean the head and shoulders.

(6) Extreme Close-Up—a picture in which the camera examines details of the subject. An extreme close-up of a person might only be a portion of the face.

Fourth, have an understanding of lighting. You do not need to be a lighting technician. However, know that differing kinds of light sources influence the reproduction of color in a picture. If adjustments are not made, an unsatisfactory picture will be delivered by the camera.

[For an explanation of color temperature, a listing of color temperatures for sun, quartz halogen, incandescent, and fluorescent lighting, and ways of adjusting cameras for these conditions, see "How Video Works" which also appears in the appendix.]

An understanding of *three-point lighting* will also better equip you. Many lighting approaches and terminologies may surface when discussing this most important element of video production. However, the basic lights in the three-point approach will always be included in lighting designs. (See illustration 24.) These three light types are discussed in relationship to a studio scene:

(1) Key Light—the main source of light which is placed slightly to the side of center at an approximate angle of 45 degrees. (See illustration 25.) This light is tilted downward about 30 degrees so as to eliminate dark eyes but not so far as to "blind" the talent. (See illustration 26.)

(2) Fill Light—a light source placed to the other side of center at an angle. This light is not as bright as the key light. Its function is to highlight details while softening harshness of the key light. Without a fill light, shadows will form on the side of the subject's face away from the key light.

(3) Back Light—light which is placed high above and behind the subject. This light points downward. By illuminating space to the rear, the subject is separated from the background. Otherwise, detail may be difficult to distinguish.

Fifth, adopt guidelines for planning quality video programming. I personally supervise numerous video productions and view works of others each year. The greatest single determinant of success in each case is not the quality of equipment, the producer's years of experience, or the amount of budget. Success is determined by the degree to which the program meets its stated objectives. A simple one-camera program, produced on a shoestring budget, may ultimately be more successful than a full-blown, multicamera production if the target audience is moved to the desired action.

The key to a successful production is *planning*. The leader responsible for a program must be willing to set aside time for detailed preproduc-

Three-Point Lighting
Illustration 24

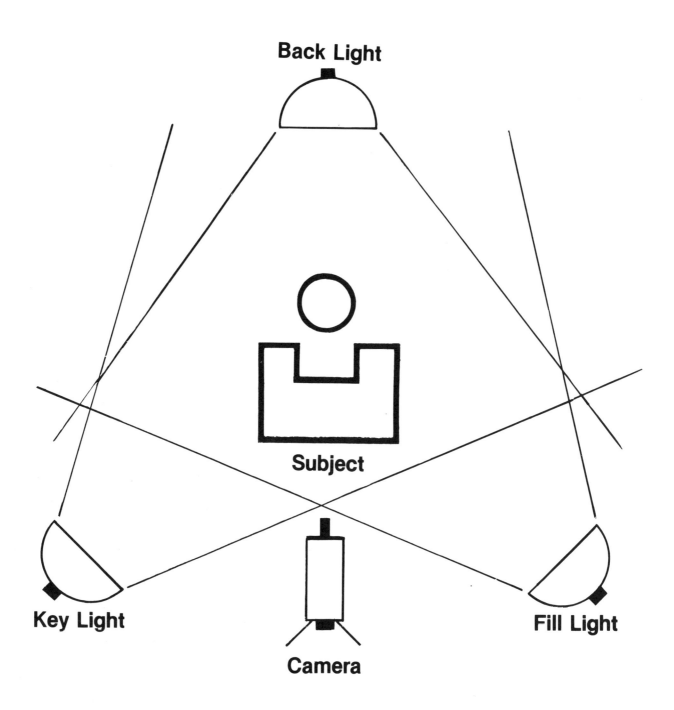

Sanctuary Lighting Diagram
Illustration 25

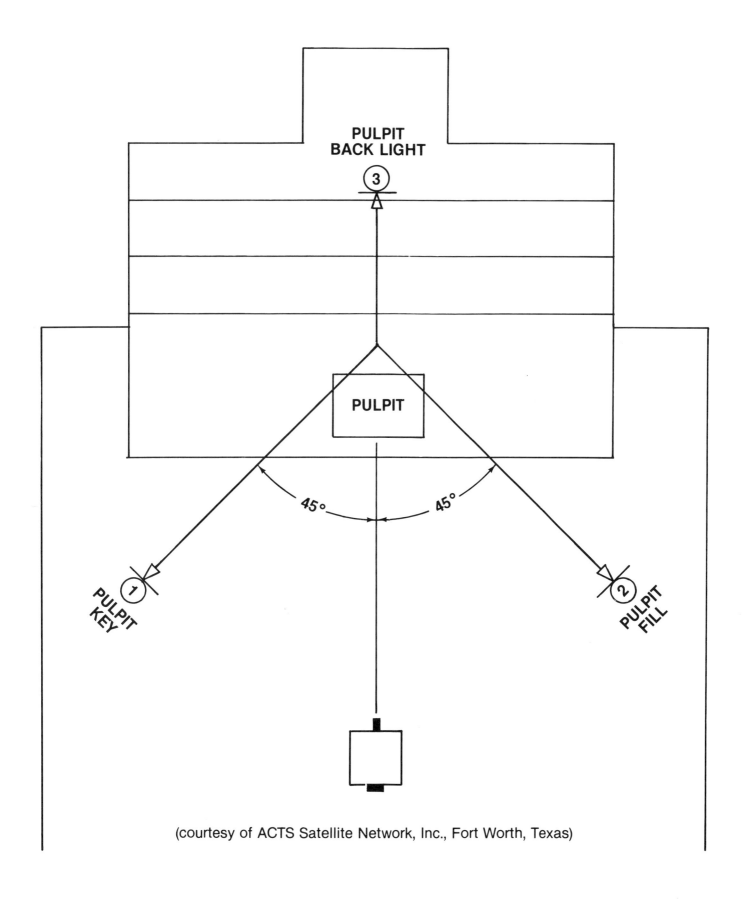

(courtesy of ACTS Satellite Network, Inc., Fort Worth, Texas)

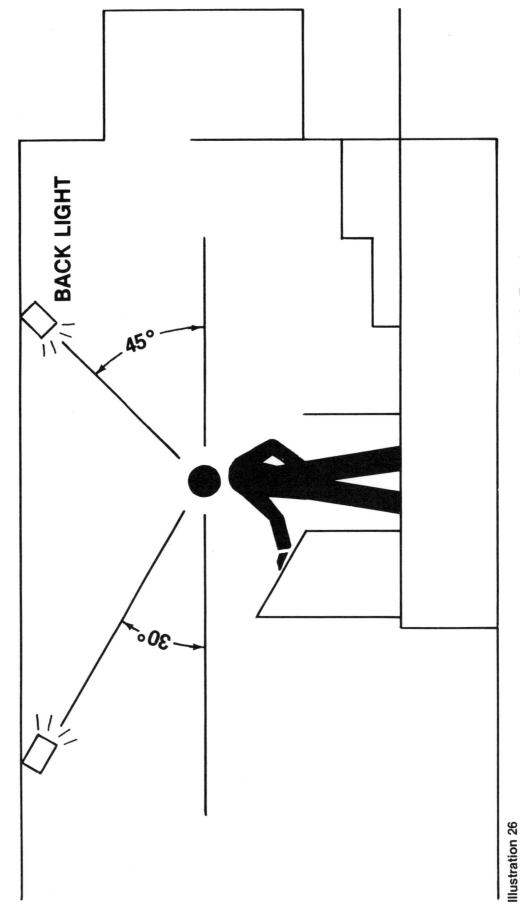

Illustration 26

Appendix F: Video Production Hints

tion planning if he expects a successful end product. A logical progression for a full, in-the-field production follows, but its principles are applicable to the smallest endeavor:

First, determine the audience and purpose. Who do you want to reach with your video message? Why do you want to reach them?

Second, analyze your audience. What do you know about this audience? What are their needs, interests, likes and dislikes, and so on?

Third, determine your measurement for success. What do you want your audience to do, once they have seen the production? What recognizable, measurable difference do you wish to see?

Fourth, begin thinking about audio and video content, the means of maintaining continuity and the way of making transitions from scene to scene.

Fifth, start script preparation with a *storyboard.* In this step, you move beyond the thinking stage to make rough sketches of proposed scenes, project preliminary camera directions, and outline dialogue. (See illustration 27.) All of this preparation is done on individual cards or sheets which, together, comprise a storyboard. (See illustration 28.) Drawings on these cards can be as rough as "stick figures" or as elaborate as finished full-color drawings. By using a storyboard of individual cards or sheets, segments can be changed to determine the proper continuity and transitions as agreed upon by the planning team.

Sixth, formalize the script. Eliminate unnecessary elements and "polish" content.

Seventh, enlist on-camera talent and assemble the technical crew.

Eighth, visit the proposed shooting site. Take thorough notes about lighting needs, sound considerations, availability of electricity, and so forth.

Ninth, secure written permission to tape in the proposed location.

Tenth, diagram the shooting site and make any necessary script adjustments based on the diagram.

Eleventh, prepare the final shooting script for use in the production. (Such a script includes proposed camera and staging directions, along with the dialogue.)

Twelfth, prepare an equipment checklist for the location shooting. (Study the sample checklist as the basis for preparing one to meet your needs.)

Video Equipment Checklist for Field Production

____ Portable Videocassette Recorders (battery operated)
____ Full-sized Videocassette Recorders (electric)
____ VCR Batteries ____ Automobile Power Adapters
____ Television Receivers/Monitors
____ Television Batteries (if TV is equipped for battery operation)
____ Rolling Equipment Rack with Switcher/SEG/Character Generator/Preview and Program Monitors
____ Cameras and Lenses ____ Viewfinders ____ Intercom Headsets
____ Camera Batteries (if camera requires batteries other than from VCR)
____ Lens Filters for Special Effects ____ Lens Caps ____ Special Application Lenses
____ Camera Cables (camera to VCR hookup)
____ Tripods ____ Tripod Heads ____ Dollies
____ Microphones: ____ Lavalier ____ Hand held ____ Shotgun ____ PZM
____ Microphone Stands: ____ Booms ____ Clips ____ Floor
____ Microphone Mixer ____ Mixer Batteries (if applicable)
____ Microphones Extension Cables ____ Batteries for Microphones (if needed) ____ Light Stands
____ Lights and Spare Lamps (at least three lights, six lamps) ____ Batteries for DC lights ____ Light Stands ____ Light Meter
____ Extension Cords (AC) Electrical Requirements ____
____ AC Master Power Cord (multiple sockets w/circuit breaker)
____ Patch Cords for Audio ____ Headphones for Sound Control
____ Hookup Cables (TV/Monitor hookup to VCR)
____ Audio Cassette Recorder with Blank Cassettes

____ Blank Videocassettes; Extra Gummed Labels and Marking Pens
____ Plugs/Cable Adapters
____ White Card/Registration Card
____ Test Equipment ____ Test Charts
____ Cleaning Kit (lens, tissue and fluid for lenses; swabs and alcohol for VCR)
____ Scripts ____ Cue Cards
____ Gaffer's Tape ____ Masking Tape
____ Edit Controller and Recorders (if needed for extended shoot)
____ Tool Kit

Thirteenth, rehearse the production under controlled conditions, such as in a studio.

Fourteenth, rehearse and tape on the shooting site.

The fourteen steps should help you in the planning process.

The sixth and final video production hint is to invest the time required to do the best job in postproduction. You may not be the one who does the editing or sound mixing. However, this most important step will "polish" the production or destroy all previous efforts. Perhaps no better video hint can be given than to urge you to make yourself readily available for creative input in postproduction. To a large extent, the success of the final product depends on a skillful job at this crucial point.

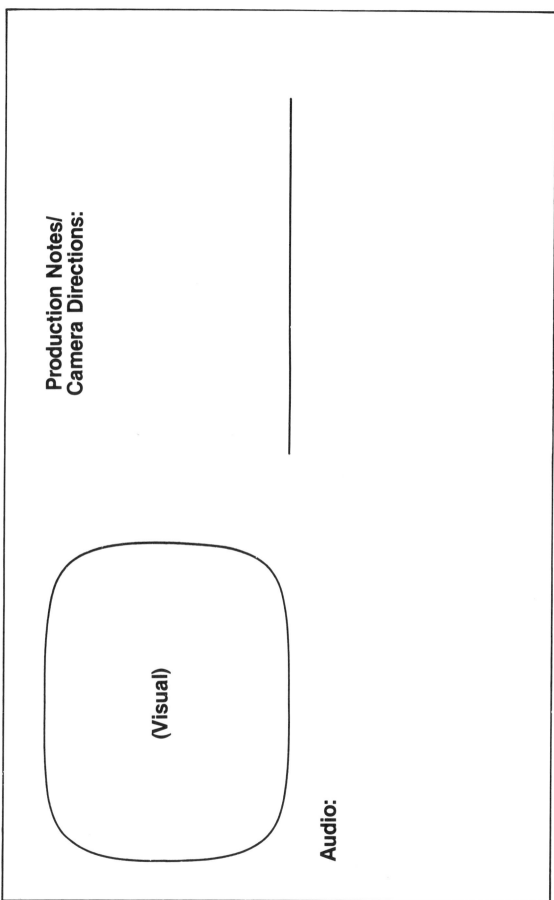

Illustration 27 — Typical Storyboard Planning Card

VIDEO   **AUDIO**   Illustration 28

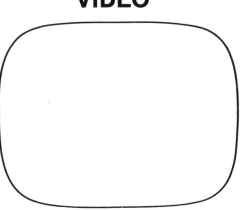

Production Notes:

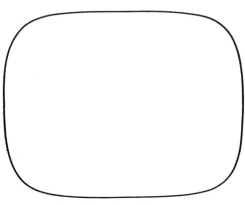

Production Notes:

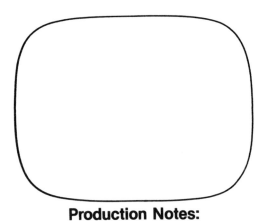

Production Notes:

Full-Sheet Storyboard Form

Appendix G:
Avoiding Copyright Infringements

Consciousness of copyrights is greater today than at any other time in the history of the country. Enactment of a completely new copyright statute in 1979 had far-reaching implications for the church, especially related to printed materials.

In the famed "Betamax Case" of the mid 1980s, the United States Supreme Court sanctioned videotaping from broadcast television for in-home use. Hailed as a landmark decision, it actually did not alter the law on taping for public performances which would include the church. Nor did the decision fully clarify the legality of taping from cable television rather than from a broadcast signal.

The above are just two examples of how the copyright law and interpretations are in a state of change. As new communications technologies continue to expand, further changes may be expected related to copyrights.

The purpose of this section of the appendix is *not* to serve as an authoritative guide on the latest copyright information—things are changing too rapidly, and the author is not a copyright attorney. Rather, the purpose is twofold: (1) to make some general observations about copyrights as they relate to educational video and cablecasting/broadcasting today, and (2) to encourage you to check the latest status of the copyright laws and their interpretations as you are involved in video usage and production.

[Note: Copyright protection extends to computer programs, too. Be certain to look for these notices at the beginning of computer software.]

Educational Video—The legality of using a copyrighted, prerecorded videotape in your church ministry depends on certain factors. When you secure a videotape from a distributor who has been granted permission to rent copyrighted programming for public performances, you are in compliance with the copyright provisions. If, on the other hand, you rent from a local or through-the-mail source whose inventory is cleared for in-home use only and who does not have the authority to grant public performance rights, you may not be in compliance with the law. So check with the person renting the tapes.

Should you record a program from broadcast television and plan to use it at church, such an application is questionable since this is not for use in your home, but rather for a public performance. Be alert to the latest copyright developments which may clarify the situation.

(It is true that educational use of broadcast video is granted under the copyright law. This application, however, seems to be for an organized educational setting rather than for an open meeting. A regular Sunday School class or a training group likely qualifies as an educational application. A worship service, fellowship, or assembly would more than likely constitute a public performance. Even in the case of an educational application, the tape may only be shown for a few days and must be erased to prevent further usage.)

In cases where you are producing educational videotapes, remember that you must have permission of the copyright holder to use copyrighted material on your tape. One of the largest usages of copyrighted material in educational video is for music—background, introduction, closing, and so on. Music publishers—even the producers of religious music—are vigorously pursuing unauthorized use of their copyrighted work. Do not find yourself in the embarrassing and illegal practice of using sheet music or prerecorded sound tracks without permission.

Be aware that there are production music collections which enable you to pay for each use of a certain selection (called a "needle drop" fee) or to purchase an entire library for unlimited use (called a "buy out"). You would be wise to secure one or both types of production collections to draw from when producing tapes.

Cablecasting/Broadcasting—Some church leaders make the mistake of assuming they are automatically covered for using copyrighted music by the cable company or television station as they produce programming on this outlet. This is not necessarily so. Moreover, purchasing sheet music or a sound track *does not* give you permission to cablecast or broadcast the music, even in the context of a regular worship service. (You are granted the right to use the music in the service but not to broadcast it unless the broadcast outlet has coverage. Moreover, receiving permission from a music-licensing agent to perform a certain musical selection with your own accompanist ("performance rights") does not grant you permission to use a prerecorded sound track of the same selection ("synchronization rights").

Given the state of copyright interpretations and legal decisions, check with your cable company or broadcast station to see if you are covered under some arrangement they have made with music-licensing agents. If they are not covering you, permission must be sought from the licensing agent each time you use copyrighted music. Costs range from no charge to a sizable amount, depending upon the copyright holder, licensing agent, your intended application for use of the music, and other factors. If the proper licensing agent is not indicated on the music, contact the publisher. Among the major music clearinghouses are:

ASCAP (The *A*merican *S*ociety of *C*omposers, *A*uthors and *P*ublishers), One Lincoln Plaza, New York, NY 10023 (212/595-3050)

BMI (*B*roadcast *M*usic, *I*nc.), 320 West 57th St., New York, NY 10019 (212/586-2000)

SESAC, Inc., 10 Columbus Circle, New York, NY 10019 (212/586-3450)

The Harry Fox Agency, Inc., 110 E. 59th St., New York, NY 10022 (212/751-1930).

Make certain that the production music collection for which you are paying "needle drop" fees or which you have "bought out" is cleared for broadcast. Many of these collections *are* cleared, but *do not* make this assumption.

The "bottom line" is: *check before using copyrighted materials!* If you are unable to obtain information locally, contact:

The Copyright Office
The Library of Congress
Washington, DC 20559
(202) 287-8700

[Note: The Copyright Office has established a "hotline" for requesting copyright forms and other literature. You may leave your request on an answering machine at any time of the day or night. The *forms hot line* may be reached by calling (202) 287-9100.]

Appendix H: Source Directory

(The following listing is not exhaustive; nor does it imply endorsement of one product over another.)

Educational Video

Religious Education Videotapes and Videodiscs

American Bible Society, 1865 Broadway, New York, NY 10023

Baptist Film Center, P. O. Box 161121, Memphis, TN 38116

Broadman Consumer Sales, 127 Ninth Ave., North, Nashville, TN 37234

Christian Video and Educational Products, P. O. Box 6883, Fort Worth, TX 76115

Christian Video Service, Box 4174, Lancaster, CA 93534

Coronet Instructional Media, 65 East South Water St., Chicago, IL 60601

Covenant Press Video, 3200 West Foster Ave., Chicago, IL 60625

CRS Video, P. O. Box 990, Dallas, TX 75221

Educator's Guide to Free Audio and Video Materials, compiled and edited by James L. Berger. Randolph, Wisconsin: Educator's Progress, Inc. (published each school year)

EcuFilm, 810 12th Ave., South, Nashville, TN 37203

Episcopal Radio-TV Foundation, 3379 Peachtree Rd., NE, Atlanta, GA 30326

Gospel Witness Films, P. O. Box 301, Atlanta, GA 30301

"In Other Words," Division of Communication, American Baptist Churches in the USA, P. O. Box 851, Valley Forge, PA 19482

International Video Bible Lessons, P. O. Box 2255, West Monroe, LA 71291

Modern Video Center, 2323 New Hyde Park Rd., New Hyde Park, NY 10042

MC-TV, First United Methodist Church, Head of Texas St., Shreveport, LA 71101

Religious Media Services, 285 Burr Rd., East Northport, NY 11731

Southern Baptist Video Tape Service, c/o Broadman Sales, 127 Ninth Ave., North, Nashville, TN 37234

Training Church Leaders Inc., 1610 LaVista Rd., Atlanta, GA 30329

United Presbyterian Church, 1940 Interchurch Center, 475 Riverside Drive, New York, NY 10115

UMCOM Video, 810 12th Ave., South, Nashville, TN 37203

Video Bible Studies, National Institute of Biblical Studies, 4001 North Dixie Highway 204, Pompano Beach, FL 33064

Video Communications, 6555 E. Skelly Dr., Tulsa, OK 74145

Video Dynamics, P. O. Box 20330, Jackson, MS 39209

Video Source Book (4th ed.), National Video Clearinghouse, Inc., 100 Lafayette Dr., Dept. REG, Syosset, NY 11791

Video Tape/Disc Guide, Religious Programs, David C. Cook Publishing Co., and the National Video Clearinghouse Inc., 1981. (The National Video Clearinghouse publishes a series of tape/disc guides on a variety of topics.)

Word, Inc., 4800 West Waco Dr., Waco, TX 76795

Books on Using Video in Education and Religious Education

Administering BTN in Your Church, compiled by Mancil Ezell. Nashville: Convention Press, 1984.

Complete Home Video Handbook by Mark Dunton and David Owen. New York: Random House, 1982.

Corporate Script Writing Book by Donna Matrazzo. Philadelphia: Media Concepts Press, 1980.

Handbook of Interactive Video, White Plains, NY: Knowledge Industry Publications, Inc.

Instructional Media by Robert Heinich. New York: John Wiley and Sons, 1982.

More Practical Video, White Plains, New York: Knowledge Industry Publications, Inc.

Nonbroadcast Television Writer's Handbook by William Van Nastran, White Plains, NY: Knowledge Industries Inc.

Off-Air Videotaping in Education; Copyright Issues, Decisions, Implications by Esther R. Sinofsky. New York: R. R. Bowker Co., 1984.

A Practical Guide to Interactive Video by Nicholas V. Iuppa. White Plains, NY: Knowledge Industry Publications, Inc.

Using Nonbroadcast Video in the Church by Daniel W. Holland, J. Ashton Nickerson and Terry Vaughn. Valley Forge, PA: Judson Press, 1980.

Video in Education and Training by James McInnes. New York: Focal Press, Inc., 1980.

Video Basics by Welby A. Smith. Alexandria, VA: Development Communications Associates, Inc., 1982.

Your Church Using BTN by Lue Bishop and Morton Rose. Nashville: Convention Press, 1983.

Magazines on Using Video in Education and Religious Education

AudioVisual Communications, United Business Communications, 475 Park Ave., South, New York, NY 10016

AV Video, Montage Publishing, Inc., 25550 Hawthorne Blvd., Suite 314, Torrance, CA 90505

Channels of Communication, Channels, Box 2001, Mahopac, New York 10541

Church Media Library Magazine, Baptist Sunday School Board, 127 Ninth Ave., North, Nashville, TN 37234

EITV: Educational and Industrial Television, C. S. Tepfer Publishing Co., Inc., 51 Sugar Hollow Rd., Danbury, CT 06810

Instructional Innovator, Association for Educational Communications and Technology (AECT), 1126 16th St., NW, Washington, D.C. 20036

International Television, The Journal of the International Television Association, Ziff Davis Publishing Co., P. O. Box 5915, Cherry Hill, NJ 08034

Media and Methods, American Society of Educators, 1511 Walnut St., Philadelphia, PA 19102

Consumer Video Magazines

(With helpful information on ½" videotape and videodiscs)

Home Video, P. O. Box 2651, Boulder, CO 80322

Video, Reese Publishing Co., Inc., P. O. Box 1116, Dover, NJ 07801

Video Review, Viare Publishing, P. O. Box 919, Farmingdale, NY 11737-001

Videoplay, C. S. Tepfer Publishing Co., Inc. 51 Sugar Hollow Rd., Danbury, CT 06810

Professional Organizations for Educational Video Users

Agency for Instructional Television, Box A, 1111 West 17th St., Bloomington, IN 47401

Association for Educational Communications and Technology (AECT), 1125 16th St., NW, Washington, DC 20036

International Television Association (ITVA), 6311 North O'Connor Rd., Suite 110, Irving, TX 75039

NAVA, International Communications Industries Assoc., 3150 Spring St., Fairfax, VA 22031

Cablecasting/Broadcasting

Religious/Family Television Networks

ACTS Satellite Network, Inc., 6350 West Freeway, Fort Worth, TX 76150

Christian Broadcasting Network, (CBN), Virginia Beach, VA 23463

Eternal Word Television Network, Inc., (EWTN), 5817 Old Leeds Rd., Birmingham, AL 35210

National Christian Network (NCN), 1150 West King St., Cocoa, FL 32922

People that Love Television Network (PTL), 7224 Park Rd., Charlotte, NC 28279

Trinity Broadcasting Network, P. O. Box A, Santa Ana, CA 92711

Appendix H: Source Directory

Books on Cablecasting/Broadcasting/LPTV/Satellite TV

Beginner's Guide to Video by David K. Matthewson: London: Newnes Technical Books, 1982.

Cablecasting Production Handbook by Joel F. Rein. Blue Ridge Summit, PA.: Tab Books, 1975.

The Communicating Church by Charles E. Swann. Atlanta, GA: Office of Media Communications, Presbyterian Church, US, 341 Ponce de Leon Ave., NE, 1981.

Creating Original Programming for Cable TV, ed. by William Drew Shaffer and Richard Wheelwright for the National Federation of Local Cable Programmers. Washington, D.C.: Communications Press, Inc., 1983.

Designing and Maintaining the CATV and Small TV Studio by Kenneth V. Knect. Blue Ridge Summit, PA: Tab Books, 1976.

Handbook for Producing Educational and Public Access Programs for Cable Television by Rudy Bretz. Englewood Cliffs, NJ: Educational Technology Publications, 1982.

How to Do Video for Evangelism by David Killer. New York: EVCOM, 105 Madison Ave., 1978.

How to Make Cable TV Work for You. Island Lake, IL: Direct Market Designs, 1982.

The Illustrated Dictionary of Broadcasts—CATV—Telecommunications by R. Terry Ellmore, Blue Ridge Summit, PA: Tab Books, 1977.

Satellite Television Handbook and Buyer's Guide by Stephen Reed. Maitland, FL: Reed Publications, 1981.

Series TV, How a Television Show is Made by Malka Drucker and Elizabeth James. New York: Clarion Books, 1983.

A Short Course in Cable by Jennifer Stearns. Saint Louis: Leadership Resources, 1981.

Small Studio Videotape Production by John Quick and Herbert Wolff. Reading, MA: Addison-Wesley Publishing Co., 1976.

Television Production Handbook by Douglas Wardwell, Blue Ridge Summit, PA: Tab Books, 1981.

The Video Pencil: Cable Communications for Church and Community by Gene Jaberg and Louis G. Wargo, Jr. New Brighton, MN: United Theological Seminary Bookstore, 3000 5th St., NW, 1980.

The Video Handbook. New York: United Business Publications, Inc., 1977.

The Video Production Guide by Lon McQuillin. Indianapolis: Howard W. Sams and Co., Inc., 1983.

Video Users Handbook by Peter Utz. Blue Ridge Summit, PA: Tab Books, 1975.

Magazines on Cablecasting/Broadcasting/LPTV/Satellite TV

*Broadcast Communications, Globecom Publishing, 4121 West 83rd St., Suite 132, Prairie Village, KS 66208

Broadcast. Broadcast Publications, Inc., 1735 DeSales St., NW, Washington, D. C. 20036

Cable Age, 1270 Avenue of the Americas, New York, NY 10020

CableVision, Titsch Publishing Co., Inc., 2500 Curtis St., Denver, CO 80205

*CommuniTV: The Magazine for Community Television Broadcasters, Globecom Publishing Limited, 4551 West 107th St., 210 Overland Park, KS 66207

*Millimeter, Millimeter Magazine, 826 Broadway, New York, NY 10003

On Cable, On Cable Publications, 25 Van Eandt St., Norwalk, CT 06855

On Location, The Film and Videotape Production Magazine, On Location Publishing, Inc., 67777 Hollywood Blvd., Suite 600, Hollywood, CA 90028

Religious Broadcasting, National Religious Broadcasters, (NRB), Box 1174, Dover, NJ 07801

Satellite TV Week, Fortuna Communications Corp., P. O. Box 308, Fortuna, CA 95540

*Telecommunications, Horizon House—Microwave, Inc., 610 Washington St., Dedham, MA 02026

Teleconference Magazine, VSN Satellite Communications Services, 5 Crow Canyon Court, Suite 209, San Ramon, CA 94583

*Television/Broadcast Communications, Globecom Publishing, Ltd., 4121 West 3rd St., Suite 265, Prairie Village, KS 66208

*Video Systems, Intertec Publishing Corp.,

P. O. Box 12912, Overland Park, KS 66212-9981

Videography, United Business Publications, 475 Park Avenue, South, New York, NY 10016

**VideoPro,* VidPro Publishing, Inc., 902 Broadway, New York, NY 10010

(*Issued at no cost to qualified persons. Contact individual publishers for more information.)

Professional Organizations for Cablecasters/Broadcasters

National Association of Broadcasters (NAB), 1771 "N" St., NW, Washington, D.C. 20036

National Cable Television Association (NCTA), 1724 Massachusetts Avenue, NW, Washington, D.C. 20036

National Federation of Local Cable Programming (NFLCP), 906 Pennsylvania Avenue, SE, Washington, D.C. 20003

National Institute for Low Power Television, 17 Washington St., Norwalk, CT 06854

National Religious Broadcasters, CN 1926, Morristown, NJ 07960

Personal Computers in Education

Church and Educational Software for Personal Computers

Bible Research System, 9414 Burnet Rd., #208, Austin, TX 78757 (Producers of "The *Word* Processor" and many others)

Cross Educational Software, P. O. Box 1536, Ruston, LA 71270

E & I Associates, 16041 Vose, Van Nuys, CA 91506

Guide to Free Computer Materials, ed. by Kathleen S. Nehner, Randolph, WI: Educators Progress Service, Inc. (Produced each school year)

"Lifewear," Word, Inc., 4800 W. Waco Drive, Waco, TX 76795

Little David Enterprises, P. O. Box 91, Fairless Hills, PA 19030

Society for Visual Education (SVE), 1345 Diversey Parkway, Chicago, IL 60614

Virginia Micro Systems, 13646 Jeff Davis Hwy., Woodbridge, VA 22191

Vision Software, Box 11131, Costa Mesa, CA 92627

Books on Personal Computers

Family Computers Under $200 by Doug Mosher. Berkeley, CA: SYBEX, Inc., 1984.

Personal Computer: A New Tool for Ministers by Russell H. Dilday, Jr. Nashville: Broadman Press, 1985.

Selecting the Church Computer by William R. Johnson. Nashville: Abingdon Press, 1984.

A 60-Minute Guide to Micro Computers by Lou Hollerbach. Englewood Cliffs, N.J.: Prentice-Hall, Inc., 1982.

Using Personal Computers in the Church by Kenneth Bedell. Valley Forge, PA.: Judson Press, 1983.

Your First Computer by Rodney Zaks. Berkeley, CA: SYBEX, Inc., 1980.

Magazines on General and Church Use of Personal Computers in Education

Christian Computing, 72 Valley Hill Rd., Stockbridge, GA 30281

Church Computer User's Network Newsletter, P. O. Box 1392, Dallas, TX 75221

Compute!, Compute! Publications, Inc., P. O. Box 5406, Greensborough, NC 27403

Computers and Electronics, Ziff Davis Publishing Co., P. O. Box 2774, Boulder, CO 80302

Electronic Education, Electronic Communications, Inc., P. O. Box 20221, Tallahassee, FL 32316

Media & Methods, American Society of Educators, 1511 Walnut St., Philadelphia, PA 19102

Personal Computing, Hayven Publishing Co., P. O. Box 2942, Boulder, CO 80322

T.H.E. (Technological Horizons in Education) Journal, Information Synergy, Inc., 1113 E. Beechwood St., Santa Ana, CA 92701

Organizations for Users of Personal Computers in the Church

Christian Computer Users Association, 1145 Alexander, SE, Grand Rapids, MI 49507

Christian Computer/based Communications, 44 Delma Dr., Toronto, Ontario M8W4N6

Church Computer Users Network, P. O. Box 1392, Dallas, TX 75221

G.R.A.P.E., P. O. Box 576, Keyport, WA 98366

Religious Computer Users Group, 7600 W. 75th St., Overland Park, KS 66024

S.O.A.R., Computer and Churches Network, 619 E. Main St., Moorestown, NJ 08057

Production Music Collections

AV Music Library, ZM Squared, 903 Edgewood Lane, Cinnaminson, NJ 08077

Creative Support Services, 1950 Riverside Drive, Los Angeles, CA 90039

DeWolfe Music Library Inc., 25 West 45th St., New York, NY 10036

Nashville Trax, Brushcreek Audio, Inc., Box 50856, Nashville, TN 37205

Omnimusic, 52 Main St., Port Washington, NY 11050

Production EFX Library, 2325 Girard St., Minneapolis, MN 55405

Soper Sound Music Library, P. O. Box 498, Palo Alto, CA 94302

The System, 1054 Cahuenga Blvd., Hollywood, CA 90038

Valentino Production Music Library, 151 West 46th St., New York, NY 10036

Manufacturers of Video Equipment

[The following addresses are provided for your convenience in contacting manufacturers for descriptive literature.]

Audio Supplies/Microphones

AKG Acoustics, Inc., 77 Selleck St., Stamford, CT 06902

Altec, 1515 South Manchester Ave., Anaheim, CA 92803

Ampex Corporation, 401 Broadway, Redwood City, CA 94063

Atlas Sound, 10 Pomeroy, Parsippany, NJ 07054

Bogen Division, Lear Siegler, Inc., P. O. Box 500, Paramus, NJ 07652

Cetec Vega, 9900 Baldwin Place, El Monte, CA 91731

Electro-Voice, Inc., 600 Cecil St., Buchanan, MI 49107

Panasonic Industrial, Co., One Panasonic Way, Secaucus, NJ 07094

RCA Corporation, Bldg. 2-2A, Camden, NJ 08102

Sennheiser Electronics, 10 West 37th St., New York, NY 10018

Shure Brothers, 222 Hartrey Ave., Evanston, IL 60204

Sony Video Communications, Sony Drive, Park Ridge, NJ 07656

Sound Masters, Inc., Route 3, Morrilton, AR 72110

Soundcraft Electronics, 1517 20th St., Santa Monica, CA 90404

Swintek Enterprises, Inc., 1180 Aster Ave., Unit J, Sunnyvale, CA 94086

Telex Communications, Inc., 9600 Aldrich Ave., South, Minneapolis, MN 55420

Wollensak/3M, 3M Center, Saint Paul, MN 55101

Cameras

Ampex Corp., 401 Broadway, Redwood City, CA 94063

GBC Corp., 74 Fifth Ave., New York, NY 10011

Hitachi Denshi America, Ltd., 175 Crossways Park West, Woodbury, NY 11797

Ikegami Electronics, 37 Brook Ave., Maywood, NJ 07607

JVC Company of America, 41 Slater Dr., Elmwood Park, NJ 07407

NEC America, Inc., Broadcast Equipment Division, 130 Martin Lane, Elk Grove Village, IL 60007

NEC Home Electronics (USA), Inc., 1401 Estes Ave., Elk Grove Village, IL 60007

Panasonic Industrial Co., One Panasonic Way, Secaucus, NJ 07094

Quasar Company, 9401 West Grand Ave., Franklin Park, IL 60130

RCA Corp., Building 2-2A, Camden, NJ 08102

Sanyo Electric, Inc., 1200 West Artesia Blvd., Compton, CA 90220

Sharp Electronics, 10 Sharp Plaza, Paramus, NJ 07652

Sony Video Communications, Sony Dr., Park Ridge, NJ 07656

Camera Lenses

Ambico, 101 Horton Ave., Lynbrook, NY 11563

Angenieux, Inc., 120 Derry Rd., Hudson, NH 03051

Buhl Optical Co., 1009 Beech Ave., Pittsburgh, PA 15233

Canon USA, Inc., 64-10 Queens Blvd., Woodside, NY 11377

Elmo Manufacturing Corp., 70 New Hyde Park Road, New Hyde Park, NY 11040

Fujinon, Inc., 672 White Plains Rd., Scarsdale, NY 10583

JVC Company of America, 41 Slater Dr., Elmwood Park, NY 07407

Panasonic Industrial Company, One Panasonic Way, Secaucus, NY 07094

Schneider Corp. of America, 400 Crossways Park Dr., Woodbury, NY 11797

Tele-Cine, Inc., 294 East Shore Ave., Massapequa, NY 11758

Tiffin Manufacturing Corp., Tiffin Professional Productions Div., 90 Oser Ave., Hauppauge, NY 11788

Character Generators

Chyron Corp. 265 Spagnoli, Melville, NY 11747

For-A Corp. of America, 49 Lexington St., West Newton, MA 02165

Knox Video Products, 8547 Grovemont Circle, Gaitherburg, MD 20877

MCI/Quantel, 3290 West Bayshore Road, Palo Alto, CA 94303

Panasonic Industrial Co., One Panasonic Way, Secaucus, NJ 07094

Portac, Inc., 108 Aero Camino, Goleta, CA 98117

QSI Systems, Inc., 12 Linscott Road, Woburn, MA 01888

Quanta Corp. 2440 South Progress Dr., Salt Lake City, UT 84119

Shintron Co., Inc., 144 Rogers St., Cambridge, MA 02142

Texscan Corp., 3102 North 29th Ave., Phoenix, AZ 85016

3M/Broadcasting Division, 3M Building, Building 2253S, Saint Paul, MN 55144

Editors—¾"

JVC Company of America, 41 Slater Dr., Elmwood Park, NJ 07407

Panasonic Industrial Company, One Panasonic Way, Secaucus, NJ 07094

Sony Video Communications, Sony Dr., Park Ridge, NJ 07656

Editors—½" VHS

Panasonic Industrial Co., One Panasonic Way, Secaucus, NJ 07094

Editors—½" Beta

Sony Video Communications, Sony Dr., Park Ridge, NJ 07656

Film Chains/Multiplexers

Buhl Optical Co., 1009 Beech Ave., Pittsburgh, PA 15233

JVC Company of America, 41 Slater Dr., Elmwood Park, NJ 07407

Kalart Victor Corp., Hultenius St., Plainville, CT 06062

Laird Telemedia, Inc., 2424 South 2570th West, Salt Lake, UT 84119

NEC America, Inc., Broadcast Equipment Division, 130 Martin Lane, Elk Grove Village, IL 60007

RCA Corp., Building 2-2A Camden, NJ 08102

Tele-Cine, Inc., 294 East Shore Dr., Massapequa, NY 11758

Telemation, Inc., 2195 South 3600th West, Salt Lake City, UT 84119

Intercom Systems

Audiotronics Corp., 7428 Bellaire Ave., P. O. Box 3997, North Hollywood, CA 94107

Bogen Division, Lear Siegler Inc., P. O. Box 500, Paramus, NJ 07652

Clear-Com Intercom Systems, 1111 17th St., San Francisco, CA 94107

Sony Video Communications, Sony Dr., Park Ridge, NJ 07656

Swintek Enterprises, Inc., 1180 Astor Ave., Unit J, Sunnyvale, CA 94086

Telex Communications, Inc., 9600 Aldrich Ave., South, Minneapolis, MN 55420

Appendix H: Source Directory

Lighting and Accessories

Acme-Lite Mfg. Co., 3401 West Madison St., Skokie, IL 60076

Anton/Bauer, Inc., One Controls Dr., P. O. Box 616, Shelton, CT 06484

Bogen Photo Corp., 17-20 Willow St., Fairlawn, NJ 07410

Colortran, 1015 Chestnut St., Burbank, CA 91502

Comprehensive Video Supply Corp., 148 Veterans Dr., Northvale, NJ 07647

Frezzolini Electronics, Inc., 7 Valley St., Hawthorne, NJ 07506

General Electric Co., Lighting Business Group, Dept. 3374, Nela Park, Cleveland, OH 44112

GTE Sylvania, Lighting Center, Danvers, MA 01923

Kliegl Brothers, 32-32 48th Ave., Long Island, City, NY 11101

Lowel-Light Mfg., Inc., 475 Tenth Ave., New York, NY 10018

Mole-Richardson Co., 937 N. Sycamore Ave., Hollywood, CA 90038

Smith-Victor Sales Corp., 301 North Colfax St., Griffith, IN 46319

Strand Century, Inc., 3411 West El Segundo Blvd., Hawthorne, CA 90250

Monitors

Audiotronics Corp., 7428 Bellaire Ave., North Hollywood, CA 91603

Conrac Corp., 600 North Rimsdale Ave., Covina, CA 91722

GBC Corp., 315 Hudson St., New York, NY 10013

Hitachi Denshi America, Ltd., 175 Crossways Park West, Woodbury, NY 11797

JVC Company of America, 41 Slater Dr., Elmwood Park, NJ 07407

NEC Home Electronics (USA), Inc., 130 Martin Lane, Elk Grove Village, IL 60007

Panasonic Industrial Co., One Panasonic Way, Secaucus, NJ 07094

RCA Corp., Building 2-2A, Camden, NJ 08102

Sharp Electronics Corp., 10 Sharp Plaza, Paramus, NJ 07652

Sony Corporation of America, Sony Drive, Park Ridge, NJ 07656

Tektronix Inc., P. O. Box 500, Beaverton, OR 97077

Videotek Inc., 125 North York St., Pottstown, PA 19464

Personal Computers

Acorn Computer Corp., 100 Unicorn Park Dr., Woburn, MA 01801

Apple Computer, Inc., 20525 Mariani Avenue, Cupterino, CA 94086

Atari, Inc., 1265 Borregas Avenue, Sunnyvale, CA 94086

Coleco Industries, Inc., 999 Quaker Lane South, West Hartford, CT 06110

Commodore Business Machines, 1200 Wilson Drive West, Chester, PA 19380

Epson America, Inc., 2780 Lomita, Torrance, CA 90505

IBM Corp., P. O. Box 1328, Boca Raton, FL 33432

Radio Shack, 1 Tandy Center, Fort Worth, TX 76102

Prompting Equipment

Cinema Products Corp., 2037 Granville Ave., Los Angeles, CA 90025

Innovative Television Equipment, 6445 DeSoto Ave., Woodland Hills, CA 91367

Q-TV Telesync, 33 West 60th St., New York, NY 10023

Telescript, 445 Livingston St., Norwood, NJ 07648

Teleskil Industries, Inc., 310-218 Blue Mountain St., Coquitlam, BC Canada V3K-4H2

Telesync Corp., 20 Insley St., Demarest, NJ 07627

Projection Video

Advent Corp., 195 Albany St., Cambridge, MA 02139

Electrohome Ltd., 809 Wellington St., North, Kitchener, Ontario, Canada N2G-4J6

Elmo Manufacturing Corp., 70 New Hyde Park Rd., New Hyde Park, NY 11040

General Electric Co., Electronics Park, Syracuse, NY 13201

Inflight Services, Inc., 485 Madison Ave., New York, NY 10022

Kloss Video Corp., 145 Sidney St., Cambridge, MA 02139

NEC Home Electronics (USA), Inc., Video Products Division, 1401 Estes Ave., Elk Grove Village, IL 60007

Panasonic Industrial Co., One Panasonic Way, Secaucus, NJ 07094

Sony Corporation of America, Sony Dr., Park Ridge, NJ 07656

Satellite Receiving Systems

Birdview Satellite Communications, Box 963, Chanute, KS 66720

Channel Master, Ellenville, NY 12428

Delta Satellite Corp., One Echo Plaza, Cedarburg, WI 53012

Dexcel, Inc., 2285C Martin Ave., Santa Clara, CA 95050

Excaliber Satellite Systems, 700 Huron St., Memphis, TN 38107

Harris Corp., Satellite Communications Division, Box 1700, Melbourne, FL 32901

Intersat Corp., 1000 Lake Saint Louis Blvd., Suite 300, Lake Saint Louis, MO 63367

KLM Electronics, Box 816, Morgan Hill, CA 95037

Scientific Atlanta, One Technology Parkway, Box 105600, Atlanta, GA 30348

Starview Systems, Box 103G, Pocahontas, AR 72455

Uniden Corp. of America, 15161 Triton Lane, Huntington Beach, CA 92649

Winegard Satellite Systems, 3000 Kirkwood St., Burlington, IA 52601

Switchers and Special Effects Generators

Adda Corp., 130 Knowles Dr., Los Gatos, CA 95030

Convergence Corp., 1641 McGaw, Irvine, CA 92714

Crosspoint Latch Corp., 316 Broad St., Summit, NJ 07901

Grass Valley Group, Inc., P. O. Box 1114, Grass Valley, CA 95945

JVC Company of America, 41 Slater Dr., Elmwood Park, NJ 07407

Knox Video Products, 8547 Grovemont Circle, Gaithersburg, MD 20877

Laird Telemedia, Inc., 2424 South 2570th West, Salt Lake City, UT 84119

MCI/Quantel, 3290 West Bayshore Rd., Palo Alto, CA 94303

Panasonic Industrial Co., One Panasonic Way, Secaucus, NJ 07094

Shintron Co., Inc., 144 Rogers St., Cambridge, MA 02142

Sony Video Communications, Sony Drive, Park Ridge, NJ 07656

Test Equipment

Hitachi Denshi America Ltd., 175 Crossways Park West, Woodbury, NY 11797

Tektronix, Inc., P. O. Box 500, Deliver Station 58-699, Beaverton, OR 97077

Texscan Corp., 3102 North 29th Ave., Phoenix, AZ 85028

Videotek Inc., 125 North York St., Pottstown, PA 19464

Time Base Correctors

Adda Corp., 130 Knowles Dr., Los Gatos, CA 95030

Ampex Corp., 401 Broadway, Redwood City, CA 94063

For-A Corp. of America, 49 Lexington St., West Newton, MA 02165

Harris Video Systems, 1255 East Arques Ave., Sunnyvale, CA 94086

Hitachi Denshi America, Ltd., 175 Crossways Park West, Woodbury, NY 11797

Microdyne Corp., P. O. Box 7213, Ocala, FL 32672

Microtime, Inc., 1280 Blue Hills Ave., Bloomfield, CT 06002

NEC America, Inc., Broadcast Equipment Division, 130 Martin Lane, Elk Grove Village, IL 60007

Tripods and Dollies

Acme-Lite Manufacturing Co., 3401 West Madison St., Skokie, IL 60076

Bogen Division, Lear Siegler, Inc., P. O. Box 500, Paramus, NJ 07652

Appendix H: Source Directory

Cinema Products Corp., 2037 Granville Ave., Los Angeles, CA 90025

Innovative Television Equipment, 6445 DeSoto Ave., Woodland Hills, CA 91367

Quick-Set, Inc., 3650 Woodhead Dr., Northbrook, IL 60062

Smith-Victor Sales Corp., 301 North Colfax St., Griffith, IN 46319

Welt/Safe-Lock, Inc., 2400 West Eighth Lane, Hialeah, FL 33010

Videocassette Recorders—¾"

JVC Company of America, 41 Slater Dr., Elmwood Park, NJ 07407

NEC Home Electronics (USA), Inc., Video Production Division, 1401 Estes Ave., Elk Grove Village, IL 60007

Panasonic Industrial Co., One Panasonic Way, Secaucus, NJ 07094

RCA Corp., Building 2-2A, Camden, NJ 08102

Sony Corporation of America, Sony Dr., Park Ridge, NJ 07656

Videocassette Recorders—½" VHS

Akai America, Ltd., 800 West Artesia Blvd., Compton, CA 90224

Hitachi Denshi America, Ltd., 175 Crossways Park West, Woodbury, NY 11797

JVC Company of America, 41 Slater Dr., Elmwood Park, NJ 07407

Magnavox, P. O. Box 6950, Knoxville, TN 37914

Mitsubishi Electronics of America, Inc., 991 Knox St., Torrance, CA 90502

NEC Home Electronics (USA), Inc., Video Products Division, 1401 West Estes Ave., Elk Grove Village, IL 60007

Panasonic Industrial Co., One Panasonic Way, Secaucus, NJ 07094

Philco, North American Phillips, P. O. Box 6950, Knoxville, TN 37914

Quasar Co., 9401 West Grand Ave., Franklin Park, IL 60130

RCA Corp., Building 2-2A, Camden, NJ 08102

Sansui Electronics Corp., 1250 Valley Grook Ave., Lyndhurst, NJ 07071

Sharp Electronics Corp., 10 Sharp Plaza, Paramus, NJ 07652

Videocassette Recorders—½" Beta

NEC Home Electronics (USA), Inc., Video Products Division, 1401 West Estes Ave., Elk Grove Village, IL 60007

Sanyo Electric, Inc., 1200 West Artesia Blvd., Compton, CA 90220

Sony Corporation of America, Sony Dr., Park Ridge, NJ 07656

Toshiba, 82 Totowa Road, Wayne, NJ 07470

Videodisc Players (Laser)

GTE Sylvania, Inc., Consumer Electronics Group, 10741 Pellicano Dr., El Paso, TX 79935

Hitachi Denshi America Ltd., 175 Crossways Park West, Woodbury, NY 11797

Pioneer Video, Inc., 200 West Grand Ave., Montvale, NJ 07645

Sony Video Communications, Sony Drive, Park Ridge, NJ 07656

Teac, 7733 Telegraph Rd., Montebello, CA 90640

Videotape Suppliers

AGFA-Gevaert, Agfa-Gevaert, Inc., 150 Hopper Ave., Waldwick, NJ 07463.

Ampex, Ampex Corp., 401 Broadway, Redwood City, CA 94063.

BASF, BASF Systems Corp., Crosby Drive, Bedford, MA 01730

DuPont, DuPont & Co., 1007 Market St., Wilmington, DE 19801.

Eastman, Eastman Kodak Co., 343 State St., Rochester, NY 14650.

Fuji, Fuji Photo Film USA, 350 Fifth Ave., New York, NY 10001.

JVC, JVC Company of America, 41 Slater Dr., Elmwood Park, NJ 07407.

Magnavox, Magnavox Electronics, Fort Wayne, IN 46804.

Maxell, Maxell Corp., 60 Oxford Dr., Moonachie, NJ 07074.

Memorex, Memorex Corp., Box 988, Santa Clara, CA 95052.

Panasonic, Panasonic Video Systems, One Panasonic Way, Secaucus, NJ 07094.

Polaroid, Polaroid, Corp., 549 Technology Square, Cambridge, MA 02139.

Sanyo, Sanyo Electric Corp., 1200 West Artesia Blvd., Compton, CA 90220

Scotch, 3M/Magnetic Tape Division, 3M Center, Saint Paul, MN 55101

Sony, Sony Corp. of America, Sony Dr., Park Ridge, NJ 07656

TDK, TDK Electronics, 755 Eastgate Blvd., Garden City, NY 11530

Teac, Teac Corp., 7733 Telegraph Rd., Montebello, CA 90640

Appendix I:
A Video Glossary

(Incorporating definitions for educational video, cablecasting, satellite television, low-power television, and computers):

A/B Rolling—a videotape editing term indicating that two videotape recorders are playing two source tapes, allowing dissolves and other special effects between the recorders as the content is blended into one tape.

Access Channels—local cable channels made available to individuals or groups by cable television operators. Though no longer required by the Federal Communications Commission (FCC), these channels are still in use in many locales. Some cities and states specify access channels in their franchising agreements. In addition to leasing an access channel, free channel space is often allocated in one to three categories: public, education, and government. Churches often may gain free or low-cost cable time on one of these access channels.

ACTS—references the ACTS Satellite Network, Inc., a religious and family-oriented network which allocates local origination programming time each day for use by churches and communities.

Addressability—capability of a cable system to send signals to specific locations or "addresses." This capability requires an addressable converter at the subscriber's end of the system. Church satellite networks such as Baptist Telecommunication Network (BTN) also use addressable equipment to deliver certain programs to preselected receiving sites. This requires an addressable decoder.

Aerial Plant—cable installed on utility poles or other similar overhead structures (see "buried plant").

Alphanumeric—information displayed on a television screen in letters and numbers by use of a character generator.

Alphanumeric Keyboard—a keyboard which allows the user to communicate with a computer in letters and numbers.

Ambience—natural background sounds which are a part of recorded audio.

Amplifier—an electronic circuit that increases the strength of an electric signal sent through it.

Angle of View—that portion of a televised scene which is visible through a particular camera lens.

Antenna—device used for sending (transmitting) or receiving communications through the air in the form of electromagnetic signals.

Antenna Gain—the effects of different types of broadcast antennas on the transmitter output power fed into them. This gain effect, multiplied by the transmitter output power, roughly determines the effective radiated power of a transmitting facility. It is possible to design high-gain antennas for meeting specific needs of an area. This is particularly useful in maximizing the impact of a low-power television transmitter. (Low-power television may be a viable outlet for local churches and religious networks.)

Antenna Pattern—the shape of a broadcast signal as it radiates from a transmitter. Transmitting antennas have different patterns such as omnidirectional (full circle), oval, and "figure eight." Choosing a transmitter with the proper transmitting pattern will maximize the signal coverage area.

Aperture—the variable opening in a lens used to control the amount of light passing through to the camera's pickup tube or focal plane. In video terms, the aperture may also be called the *iris*.

Arbitron—a research firm which gathers audience response data for radio and television and which conducts special studies for the broadcast industry. Arbitron is one of the major companies whose data determines television ratings.

Arc—(1) movement of a video camera in a circular pattern around the subject; (2) an imaginary, circular pattern in which communications satellites hover at 22,300 miles above the equator.

Area of Cable Influence—the geographic area served by a particular cable company.

Area of Dominant Influence (ADI)—the geographic area where a television station achieves its greatest audience. As used by Arbitron, *ADI* is a term denoting an area where a television station can effectively deliver an advertiser's message to a majority of the homes.

ASCAP—An acronym for the *A*merican *S*ociety of *C*omposers, *A*rtists and *P*ublishers, one of the music-licensing organizations responsible for granting permission and collecting fees for use of copyrighted music.

ASCII—acronym for the *A*merican *S*tandard *C*ode for *I*nformation *I*nterchange, the code used in personal computers for representing letters and numbers as patterns of bits.

Assemble Editing—a method of editing a videotape in which various taped segments are retaped in a new sequence to form a coherent whole.

Attenuate—to reduce or turn down the level of a signal.

Audience—the number or percentage of people exposed to a television program.

Audience Composition—the definition of an audience by age, sex, education, income, etc.

Audio—(1) sound; (2) the sound portion of a video production.

Audio Dub—rerecording the audio portion of a videotape while retaining the video portion of the signal.

Audio Head—the recording and playback mechanism for sound on a video or audio recorder. In the record mode, it receives an audio signal and transfers it onto the passing magnetic tape, thus storing it as a magnetic impulse. In the playback mode, the head reproduces sound from magnetic impulses as picked up from the passing magnetic tape.

Audio In—an input jack or receptacle on a piece of equipment which receives an audio signal from an outside source.

Audio Level—the strength of an audio signal.

Audio Mixer—an electrical device which accepts a number of audio signals and combines them into one total signal.

Audio Out—an output jack which delivers an audio signal from a piece of equipment. By plugging into this jack, the audio signal may be carried to another piece of equipment.

Audio Track—the particular area on an audio or videotape which carries audio information.

Auto Assemble—computer-operated videotape editing. Editing decisions are entered into the computer, and edits are then made unaided by the operator.

Automated Channel—a cable channel dedicated to providing information in alphanumeric or graphic form via a character generator. Some examples are: news, weather, church and community bulletin boards, stock market reports, and real estate listings.

Automatic Gain Control (AGC)—an electronic circuit that regulates an incoming signal—audio or video—to a predetermined level.

Automatic Iris—a feature on some video cameras which automatically adjusts the aperture (iris) of a lens in response to the light level in the scene being shot.

Availability—commercial time that a cable system, broadcast station, or network has for sale.

Available Light—the amount of lighting present for videotaping a scene. Taping with available light usually means that no additional lighting is brought in for making the recording.

Azimuth—the compass direction from due north, measured in degrees. In mounting a satellite dish antenna, true north must be used, so a local correction for magnetic deviation is necessary. (Consult a local airport for this deviation from true north.)

Azimuth-Elevation Mount—a satellite dish antenna mount and aiming system. It pivots in two directions, one pivot allowing horizontal rotation about the azimuth angle from due north and the other pivot allowing elevation above the horizon.

Backlight—illumination (lighting) from behind

a subject and opposite the camera to help define the subject from its background.

Backspacing—rewinding a videotape slightly in preparation for making an edit. Many video recorders do a backspace edit each time the unit is placed in the record mode, thus eliminating a picture breakup between scenes.

Backup—a copy or duplicate of a computer disk.

Bandwidth—the signal frequency range which a piece of equipment can encode or decode.

Barndoor—the metal flap mounted in front of a spotlight to control the spread of the light beam.

Basic—an acronym for *B*eginners *A*ll-purpose *S*ymbolic *I*nstruction *C*ode, a high-level computer language found on many small computers.

Basic Cable—the service which cable subscribers receive for the base fee every month. Movie channels and other services may require payment above the basic cable rate.

Batten—the pipes on which lighting fixtures are hung.

Baud—a measurement of speed for transmitting computer data. It is based on bits per second.

Beam—the stream of electrons emitted by an electron gun in a video camera tube or in a television picture tube.

Beam Width—the angle of sky which can be picked up by a satellite dish antenna. Large dishes have narrow beam widths which reduce noise (audio and video interference) from its sides while small dishes have wider beam widths and are noisier.

Beta—also known as Betamax, this half-inch videocassette format was developed by Sony and is not interchangeable with half-inch VHS.

Bidirectional Mike—a microphone which accepts sound waves from two opposite directions while diminishing soundwaves from other directions.

Bird—a colloquial term for a communications satellite.

Bit—a computer term for one or two digits (*bi*nary digi*t*). This references data in a form used by computers. All data can be reduced to bits, the smallest unit of information used by a computer. It represents an "on" or "off" position in a computer memory.

Black Level—the electronic signal level defined as representing black in a television picture.

Block Programming—a series of back-to-back programs with similar appeal.

Blooming—distortion of a television picture caused by a high video level or excessively bright spot in a scene being taped.

BMI—an acronym for *B*roadcast *M*usic *I*ncorporated (similar to ASCAP). BMI is a music-licensing agency.

BNC—a professional-type video connector which requires a push and twist to securely lock the pieces being joined together.

Boom—a long arm or crane holding a microphone or camera.

Boom Up; Boom Down—the command to raise or lower the boom arm holding a microphone.

Booting—running a preliminary program on a computer to make it ready to operate.

Break—time between or within a program which is used for commercials, announcements, or newsbriefs.

Brightness—the measure of how bright an object appears on television.

BTN—an acronym for *B*aptist *T*elecommunication *N*etwork, a satellite-delivered, denominational network of information and inspiration for leaders and members of local churches.

Bug—an error in a computer program which prevents it from working correctly, if at all.

Bulk Eraser—a device used to erase audio or videotape by producing a strong magnetic field near the tape.

Bump—to transfer or dub from one videotape or channel to another. The term is often used when dubbing from a smaller tape such as VHS (½″) to ¾″ or ¾″ to 1″.

Buried Plant—the installation of cable underground (see aerial plant).

Burn-In—Image retention by a camera pickup tube, caused by an excessively bright subject or by photographing a static scene for an extended period (also called "lag").

Bus—an electronic pathway, along which data travels from one or more sources to one or more destinations.

Busy—a television picture which is too cluttered.

Byte—a computer term for a set of eight bits, considered as one unit. It represents one letter, number, or instruction.

Cable Penetration—the proportion of all television homes (homes with at least one television set) in an area that subscribes to cable.

Cable Ready—describes a television set or video recorder which will tune in cable channels (midband frequencies) as well as over-the-air broadcast channels.

Cablecasting—programming other than broadcast signals which is produced and carried on cable systems.

Cable System—the actual cable company plant with its four components: (1) Headend—where television signals are received via satellite, microwave, or television antennas and retransmitted through the cable system. (2) Trunk lines—the major cable lines taking signals from the headend to the community via large cables and periodic signal amplifiers. (3) Feeder lines—cables which go from the trunk line to directly past homes. (4) Drop lines—cables which branch from the feeder lines into the homes.

Camcorder—a term by Panasonic for a combination video camera and recorder. The single unit is relatively lightweight and uses ½" videotape which runs at much higher speeds than consumer ½", thus yielding a superior picture. The Camcorder is in the VHS format. Many broadcast stations are using these units to gather news and to do field production. (Similar units are also available in the Beta format—Betacam—as well as other configurations and sizes.)

Cameo—the lighting technique of "suspending" a person or object in space by using a black background and spotlighting the subject.

Camera—a device capable of receiving images as reflected light through a lens system, converting these images into electric impulses from the television pickup tubes, and passing them on to a recorder, monitor, or switching device.

Camera Control Unit (CCU)—a separate unit containing controls for regulating certain camera functions. It is usually located near other control equipment such as the switcher, monitors, recorders, and so forth.

Capstan—a motor-driven rotating metal shaft in an audio or video recorder that governs the speed of the tape passing through the machine. The tape is sandwiched between the capstan and a rubber pinch roller. As the capstan rotates at the proper speed, the tape is pulled with the precision needed for recording and playback.

Cardioid Mike—a microphone which picks up sound waves in a heart-shaped pattern—from the sides and front—while rejecting sounds from the rear.

Cathode-ray Tube (CRT)—a vacuum tube which produces a series of electrons that are focused into a beam. The beam is directed down the length of the tube where the electrons strike a phosphorus coating on the base of the tube, making it glow. Also called a *picture tube*.

CATV—an acronym for *Community Antenna Television*: cable television.

CBN—an acronym for the Christian Broadcasting Network, a twenty-four-hour religious and family programming service.

CCD—an acronym for *charge coupled device*, a small light-sensitive, integrated circuit or chip used in a videocamera in place of the pickup tube to produce a video signal. Light falling on the CCD is translated into an electrical charge. Using a CCD can reduce the size and weight of videocameras.

CCTV—closed-circuit television.

Channel Capacity—in a cable television system, the number of channels which can be carried simultaneously.

Character Generator—a device which electronically produces lettering and graphic displays onto a television screen for use in video production.

Chip—an integrated circuit.

Chroma Key—a special video effect wherein a camera is adjusted so it will not record anything that is a certain color, usually blue or green. By placing a subject in front of a blue or green background, this subject can then be superimposed over another scene, giving the appearance of one composite picture.

Closed Circuit—a television program distributed to specific receivers but not telecast to the public.

Appendix I: A Video Glossary

Coaxial Cable—a round, television transmission line consisting of a single center wire and an outer braid or foil separated by nonconductive material. Often called "coax," it is used in all types of antenna systems, cable systems, and video production.

Cobol—an acronym for *Common Business Oriented Language*, a computer language for business applications.

Color Bars—the standard color test signal for television which contains samples of primary and secondary colors, plus black and white. Color bars are placed at the beginning of videotapes to allow operators to adjust playback equipment to receive proper color rendition.

Color Temperature—the relative degree of color quality produced by a given light source, measured in "degrees Kelvin." This measurement generally refers to the amount of red and blue in "white" light. Color temperature is important when matching proper camera setting to lighting conditions or the color will be distorted in the picture. Cameras determine color on how they "see" white.

Comet Tailing—a streaking in the television picture caused by movement of a bright light source leaving an image on the pickup tube.

Command—an instruction which tells a computer what to do. Grouped together, these commands constitute a program.

Communications Satellite—a vehicle in stationary orbit 22,300 miles over the equator which receives and transmits audio and video signals used by cable systems and others involved in telecommunications.

Compatibility—the ability of one piece of video equipment to play through or with another piece of equipment. Two recorders are compatible if video signals can be duplicated from one machine to another with cables. This ability does not necessarily make the two machines interchangeable. For instance, VHS, Beta, and ¾" recorders are compatible since their video signals are all produced in the same manner. But they are not interchangeable.

Composite Signal—a complete picture signal containing video information as well as a sync (synchronization) pulse.

Computer—a machine which receives data, processes it, and supplies a result to the user. The basic parts of a computer are: the central processing unit (CPU), memory, and input/output circuits.

Construction Permit—the final step in pursuing approval for a low-power or full-power television station. The permit is granted by the Federal Communications Commission. The permit allows one year for activity to begin by the applicant.

Continuity—the flow of action and sound within a video production, moving smoothly from one scene to another.

Contour—the theoretical coverage area of a broadcast station. Each television station has three contours: Grade B (good signal; largest coverage area), Grade A (better signal; smaller area) and City Grade (best signal; smallest area).

Cursor—a flashing light or indicator showing where the next data is to be entered into a computer.

Cut—(1) an editing or production term for making an instantaneous transition from one picture to another; (2) stopping all action after videotaping.

Cut-In—an insert from another source which is introduced into a video program.

Cutaway—a video shot which focuses on a view other than the principal action, such as a cutaway to an audience shot during a concert or a cutaway to an item being discussed during an interview.

Cutoff List—before a construction permit is granted for a local television station, the Federal Communications Commission makes public any applications for licenses. Other competing applications may be filed within the specified time period before the cutoff for applications is reached. This procedure is being used widely in the granting of low-power television station licenses.

Cyclorama (Cyc)—a continuous piece of curtain fabric which runs around the edges of a studio, used to produce an illusion of an infinite depth. The cyc may be "painted" with colored light to create a variety of effects.

Daisy Wheel—a type of computer printer which

uses a circular disc with spokes resembling a flower with petals. Impressions are made by a hammer striking the appropriate spoke containing the desired letter or number. Daisy wheel printers yield impressions similar to a typewriter and are often referred to as "letter quality printers." Daisy wheel printers cannot reproduce graphics.

Data—basic information which can be processed by computer—any number, letter, symbol, or group of the same.

dB—an abbreviation for *decibel,* a unit for measuring levels of sound and electrical signals.

DBS—an acronym for *Direct Broadcast Satellite,* a high-powered satellite transmission service which delivers its signal directly to the viewer's home by its own relatively small satellite dish, not through a cable system. Because of high power requirements of DBS, less channels are generally offered than on a regular communications satellite.

Debug—the process of removing a "bug" or flaw from a computer program.

Decoder—a device for descrambling (or decoding) an electronically encoded television signal into a viewable signal with correct sound. Decoders are necessary for receiving some cable and satellite-delivered programs.

Dedicated Channel—a cable channel devoted to carrying a single programming source such as a network.

Default—the value automatically assigned to something in a computer program if the person using the program does not assign a value.

Depth of Field—the distance between the nearest object in focus and the most distant object in focus as viewed through a particular lens. Depth of field is determined by distance from the subject to the camera, focal length of the lens, and the aperture or f-stop setting of the camera. The larger the aperture opening, the greater the depth of the field.

Designated Market Area (DMA)—definition by the A. C. Nielsen Company of a geographic market area where a television station has its greatest audience.

Dew Control—a video recorder warning indicator that there is too much moisture in the air for safe operation.

Dimmer—a control for adjusting the brightness of light.

Diapole—(1) an antenna element in the feedhorn of a satellite receiving system which collects the television signal and passes it on to the low noise amplifier (LNA); (2) a UHF television antenna.

Director—the person in a television production who coordinates all elements of the program.

Directory—an index to data on a computer disk.

Disc—a flat, circular object upon which prerecorded television programming is stored. This material is retrieved by a videodisc player.

Dish—the component of a satellite receiving system which initially receives the satellite signal. This dish-shaped device is also known as a *parabolic antenna.*

Disk/Diskette—a flat, circular plate of plastic or aluminum which is covered with magnetizable material. This disk is used to store and retrieve computer data by means of magnetic impulses in a similar manner to recording tape.

Disk Drive—the hardware used to record and retrieve information from a computer disk. A motor spins the disk as a read/write head moves across the disk surface, playing back ("reading") or recording ("writing") data.

Dissolve—gradually fading from one video picture to another with a brief overlap.

Distribution Amplifier—an amplifier for video and/or audio which accepts an input signal and provides multiple outputs at the same level. A distribution amplifier is helpful when "feeding" several video recorders from one single source such as another video recorder or satellite receiver.

Dolly—(1) a rolling support for a camera; (2) a command to move a videocamera in toward the subject ("dolly in") or away from the subject ("dolly out").

Dot Matrix—a type of computer printer which prints characters as a set of small dots in a grid pattern or matrix. Dot matrix printers are also capable of printing graphics.

Downconverter—that portion of a satellite receiving system which changes the high frequency

Appendix I: A Video Glossary

microwave signal from the satellite to a lower frequency.

Downlink—(1) the communications signal from a satellite to a TVRO (*Te*le*V*ision *R*eceiver *O*nly "dish"); (2) that part of a satellite transmission system from the satellite to the ground.

Drop-out—loss of part of the video signal during playback because of a lack of magnetic coding on a portion of the tape or foreign matter on the tape such as dirt or grease.

Dub—to copy audio and/or video from one recording to another.

Dupe—an abbreviation for duplicate. It means a copy of a tape made from an original or a copy of an original.

Dynamic Microphone—a highly pressure-sensitive microphone featuring a moving coil with either a unidirectional or omnidirectional pickup pattern.

Earth Station—a dish-shaped, satellite antenna and accompanying equipment for receiving satellite signals. (Some such antenna systems are also designed to transmit signals to communications satellites. These are more costly units.)

Editing—(1) in a computer, correcting or changing data prior to sending it to the processor; (2) in audio or video, to do away with undesired content and to build a desired sequence. Video is edited electronically by taping segments onto a new tape. Audio may be edited electronically or by physically cutting out and rejoining the tape. (Do *not* cut videotape.)

EFP—an acronym for *E*lectronic *F*ield *P*roduction, using video equipment on location to do production similar to a film crew, usually with one camera and recorder.

Eight Pin Connector—a commonly used plug for joining a video-recorder and a monitor with all audio and video connectors, including ground and sync (synchronization) signal.

Electret Condenser Microphone—a sensitive, capacitor-driven microphone which uses a DC power supply.

Electron Gun—the assembly at the end of a television picture tube or a video camera pickup tube. This gun produces an electron beam for scanning the television picture tube or the target area of a camera pickup tube.

Electronic Viewfinder—a small television screen on a video camera which allows the camera person to see exactly what is being captured by the camera. These viewfinders usually produce black-and-white images.

Elevation—a measurement in degrees of height above the horizon with zero being the horizon and ninety degrees being directly overhead. Angles of elevation are used in the process of aiming a satellite dish antenna.

Encoder—a scrambler; device used to break up television signals into parts. The signal must pass through a decoder at the receiving end to put the signal back into a usable form.

ENG—an acronym for *E*lectronic *N*ews *G*athering, using a battery-operated video camera and recorder together to gather news quickly and efficiently.

EPROM—an acronym for *E*rasable, *P*rogram, *R*ead-*O*nly *M*emory, a memory which can be programmed and erased by the computer operator.

Erase Head—the electromagnetic device on an audio or video recorder which, when activated, erases electronic information on the magnetic tape.

Essential Area—the portion of a television picture which is seen on almost all receivers (television sets) and monitors, regardless of size or adjustment. Vital information in any video production should fall within the central portion of the screen known as the essential area.

Establishing Shots—usually a long (wide) shot by a video camera which orients the viewer to the surroundings where the scene will be taking place.

F-Connector—one of the most common screw-on-type fittings for making video connections. F-connectors are usually found on the end of the wire provided by the cable company to the subscriber.

F-Stop—a number indicating the size of the opening of a lens aperture. The larger the f-stop number, the smaller the opening in the aperture, thus allowing little light to pass on to the camera pickup tube. The smaller the f-stop, the larger the opening.

Fade—(1) decreasing a video signal to black ("fade to black") or gradually revealing a picture from black ("fade in"); (2) decreasing audio volume to silence.

FCC—an acronym for *F*ederal *C*ommunications *C*ommission, the federal regulatory agency for television broadcasting/cablecasting with headquarters in Washington, DC.

Feed—transmission of a signal from one program source to another such as a network feed, remote feed, or satellite feed.

Feedhorn—the component of a satellite-receiving system which takes the signal from the parabolic antenna (dish) and passes it on to the Low Noise Amplifier (LNA).

Field—(1) in video, half of a video picture representing one pass of the electron beam over the surface of the television tube, covering 262.5 lines. With one additional pass, the two fields compose a frame of video. (Though it takes two passes of the electron beam to compose a frame of video, the human eye does not work as rapidly, and the two passes "blend" into one whole picture.) (2) In computers, a collection of related data or part of a complete record.

File—a collection of work on a computer disk which is given a name and/or a number.

Fill Light—the secondary light source applied to a subject to eliminate or soften shadows in a video scene caused by the key light (see also "back light" and "key light").

Film Chain—a device for transferring films, slides, and other projected visuals to videotape. The projected images are focused into a series of lenses. The video camera is then placed on the other end of this lens series where an image enters the camera lens and onto the camera's pickup tube for recording.

Flowchart—a computer term for a graphic illustration of a computer program—its flow.

Fluid Head—a video camera support at the top of a tripod which utilizes a fluid cushion to make a camera move smoothly.

Focal Length—in video, the distance from the optical center of the lens to the pickup tube of the camera.

Focus—the point where light rays meet to produce a clear, sharp, and well-defined image. This is accomplished on a camera by adjusting the lens.

Footcandle—a measure of light intensity based on illumination received by a surface one foot from a lighted candle; hence one footcandle. Video cameras are rated to work with a certain number of footcandles. The metric equivalent is "lux" with one footcandle equalling 10.76 lux. Also, one footcandle equals one lumen per square foot.

Footprint—(1) satellite coverage area; (2) a map showing the signal strength of a communications satellite in different parts of the country. A footprint helps to determine the size and quality of satellite receiving equipment needed to utilize a satellite signal in various locations. Since American communications satellites are focused on the Midwest, the greater the distance from this point, the greater size of dish and quality of equipment needed to receive an adequate signal.

Format—(1) in video, a grouping of videocassette recorders by videotape width, size of cassette (if any), method of recording and signal system; (2) in computers, the arrangement or layout of data on the screen, in a file, or on paper.

Fouled Heads—dirty video heads caused by conductive material filling the gap in the electromagnets (or heads).

Frame—a complete 525-line television picture composed of two 262.5-line fields which takes one-thirtieth of a second to scan (see "field").

Franchise—in cable, the agreement between a cable operator and a governmental body defining responsibilities, rights, and boundaries for a cable system operating in a certain locale. The governmental body is usually on a city or county level.

Freeze-Frame—to stop the action on a single video frame. Many video recorders have a freeze-frame capability.

Frequency—the number of complete cycles per second of an electrical signal, expressed in hertz (Hz). One hertz equals one cycle per second.

Gaffer's Tape—a two-inch-wide tape similar to duct tape which is used in video productions to hold items together, to wrap shiny objects for elimination of reflections, etc. Gaffer's tape is superior to duct tape because it does not leave a gummy residue upon removal.

Gain—the amount of signal amplification for audio and video, expressed in decibels (dB's). "Riding gain" means watching and varying controls to produce proper sound and video levels.

Gels—colored sheets of translucent plastic used for filtering and coloring light from spotlights. These filters were originally made from gelatin, hence the name "gels."

Generation—the amount of distance from an original videotape. The original is the "first generation" or "master." A copy of the original is "second generation," a copy of the copy is "third generation," and so on.

Geostationary Orbit—first described by Arthur C. Clark, this orbit at 22,300 miles above the equator enables a satellite to revolve around the earth once every twenty-four hours. A satellite appears to be stationary above the earth at this altitude and has access to one third of the earth's surface.

Ghost—a double image on the television screen caused by a signal reflection in a poor reception area.

Gigahertz—a term used to indicate frequency. One gigahertz is one billion cycles per second. Satellite downlink signals are assigned frequencies in the four-gigahertz (GHz) band (3.7GHz to 4.2GHz).

Glitch—a visual breakup in the video signal. It may be seen as a narrow horizontal bar moving vertically through the picture or as a more momentary distortion.

Graphic Tablet—an instrument for entering data into a computer in a pictorial form. The picture is drawn on the tablet's surface with a stylus. A sensing mechanism of the tablet enables the computer to translate this input into coordinates for locating purposes.

Hard Copy—computer printouts on paper.

Hardware—the actual, physical video equipment such as cameras, recorders, and so forth, or computer equipment such as printers, monitors, keyboards.

HDTV—an acronym for *High Definition Television*. This new generation of television makes it possible for pictures to have more clarity and less graininess. Rather than the 525 lines of resolution of a traditional television set, HDTV offers approximately 1,000 lines of resolution. HDTV may also include improvement in sound quality (stereo) and color.

Head—an electromagnetic assembly for recording onto or retrieving signals from a magnetic medium such as an audiotape, videotape, or computer disk.

Headend—the location where a cable system receives its signal via satellite and television antennas, amplifies the signals, converts them to specific channel frequencies, and sends them on to subscribers.

Hertz—a unit of frequency indicating the number of cycles per second. One hertz equals one cycle per second.

Hologram—a three-dimensional television image made by the conversion of two laser beams.

Homes Passed—the number of homes which have the potential for being hooked up to a cable system since they are passed by the cable company's feeder line.

Image Retention—a video camera's pickup tube retaining an image after the camera is focused on something else. This usually results from shooting a bright light source (also called "lag").

In the Can—a colloquialism for completed television program ready for showing at any time.

Initialization—the procedure for preparing a computer disk to store data.

Insert Edit—a type of video editing in which the existing control track of one videotape is maintained and new video and/or audio can be inserted without disturbing the material before and after the edit.

Instruction—a single line of computer program telling the computer to perform a certain function.

Interactive Cable—two-way cable, making it possible for subscribers to send information back through the cable system. Some applications are: shopping at home, audience-response polls, banking by cable, burglar and fire alarms monitored by cable, and video games provided for a fee and changed each month.

Interactive Video—equipment capable of getting a response from a user and then selecting additional information for display in accord with the user's response. (Video recorders, videodisc players—especially laser-operated videodisc players—and computers are being combined to produce meaningful, interactive learning experiences.)

Interchangeability—the capability to exchange tapes between videorecorders of the same format and to have these tapes play properly. (For instance, tapes from two VHS recorders are interchangeable. Though both are half-inch tape, VHS and Beta tapes are not interchangeable.)

Interconnection—the joining of two or more cable systems for mutual distribution of programs. The systems may be joined by coaxial cable, microwave, satellite, or other means.

IPS—*an acronym for inches per second*, indicates the speed of audio or videotape during recording of playback.

Iris—(See "aperture.")

Jitter—movement in a television picture caused by a lack of synchronization.

Joy Stick—a computer input device used to move a dot on the monitor or CRT. It is most commonly employed for computer games.

Kelvin—the scientific measuring scale in degrees by which color temperature of a light source is measured.

Key Light—the main source of light on a subject or scene. The light is placed to the front and slightly to the side of the object being taped at a 45° angle.

Keyboard—the most common input device for computers.

Kilobyte—abbreviate *K*, it is 1,024 bytes. It is the unit of measuring computer memory. For instance, many personal computers have 64K.

Kilohertz—1,000 hertz or cycles per second.

Language—a consistent method of communicating instructions to a computer in unambiguous terms.

Laserdisc—a type of videodisc player which utilizes a laser beam to "read" information in pits on the disc and introduce it as a television picture with sound. Laser discs have a virtually unlimited life expectancy since nothing touches them during the playback process, unlike some other videodiscs which use a stylus similar to a record player. Laserdiscs can also be used effectively in interactive video since reference numbers are encoded on the disc as part of the signal.

Lavalier Mike—a small microphone designed to be worn around the neck or clipped to clothing near the neck.

Leased Channel—any cable channel made available by the operator for a fee.

Letter Quality Printer—a computer printer which produces high-quality print.

Level—the strength of an audio or video signal.

Licensee—a person or organization granted a license by the Federal Communications Commission.

Light—reflected energy.

Light Pen—a computer input device used with a monitor or CRT.

List—sequential statements which make up a computer program.

Live—a broadcast or cablecast which is transmitted as it happens.

Load—to call up data on a program from a computer storage device like a disk or tape and place it in the computer's memory for usage.

Local Origination Programming—program material produced by the local cable company or others which focuses on community events. Churches have a tremendous opportunity to gain goodwill and reach people by becoming producers of local origination programming.

Log—a moment-by-moment accounting of the day's program schedule. Radio and television stations always maintain a log.

LNA—an acronym for low noise amplifier, that component of a satellite-receiving system which amplifies the weak signal from the feedhorn and sends it to the receiver.

Low-Power Television (LPTV)—a relatively new class of television station which operates at greatly reduced power as compared to full-power stations. Transmitters are generally within the 100-to-1000-watt range. Both the coverage area (perhaps a twenty-five-mile diameter) and the start-up costs are significantly less than for full power. LPTV stations are similar to translators which have been used for years to receive and retransmit full power television station signals in remote locations. However, LPTV stations can originate their own programs. The FCC "must carry" rules do not apply to LPTV. (See "must carry.")

Lumen—(see "footcandle.")

Luminance—(1) a value assigned to an object, based on its brightness; (2) the brightness of a television picture.

Magnetic Tape—a thin plastic ribbon coated with iron oxide particles which, when magnetized by an audio or video record head, will record for later playback (audio and/or video). Similarly, computer disks are plastic or aluminum coated with iron oxide particles. The head in the disk drive records and receives data.

Master—an original videotape or audiotape. The edited master is the tape onto which a program has been edited.

Master Control—the room where all video and audio of various production studios are fed for distribution and recording.

MATV—an acronym for *Master Antenna Television System*, a system serving a number of television sets from one central antenna. Many apartment complexes use MATV.

Megabyte—approximately one million bytes.

Megahertz—one million cycles per second.

Memory—the portion of a computer system where data is stored.

Menu—a listing of all tasks which can be performed by a computer program. The menu is displayed on the computer's CRT (or monitor) and each option is assigned a letter or number. Pressing the appropriate key exercises one of the options.

Microcomputer—a relatively inexpensive, desktop computer with memory of 128K or less (see "kilobyte").

Microwave Relay System—a means of transmitting television and other high-frequency signals via microwaves. Each microwave link (relay station) must have line of sight (unobstructed path) to the next link. Microwave "dishes" on towers are common sights in most communities, especially near radio and television stations, telephone company facilities, and other communication installations. A mobile microwave dish mounted on a truck or van allows television stations to do live reporting back to the studio. (Microwave transmitters must be licensed by the Federal Communications Commission.)

Mike (MIC)—microphone.

Minicomputer—a larger, faster, and more powerful unit than a microcomputer. The minicomputer has several hundred K of memory (see "kilobyte").

Mix—(1) in video, to blend the picture and sound tracks; (2) in audio, to blend two or more sound channels.

Mobile Unit—a technical center in a truck or van that allows video production away from the studio. This is also called a "remote unit."

Modeling Light—(see "key light.")

Modem—an acronym for *Modulation/Demodulation*, a device making it possible for computers to communicate over telephone lines.

Modulator—the component of a satellite-receiving system which adapts the signal from the microwave receiver into one of the channel frequencies on a regular television set. (See also "RF modulator.")

Monitor—a television set having no receiving circuitry or tuner, used to display video signals from a video camera, video recorder, and so forth. Also, monitors are used with computers, sometimes with higher-resolution screens to make it easier to read small print.

Monochrome—black and white.

Multiple System Operator (MSO)—a company which owns and operates more than one cable system. Most local cable companies are owned by MSO's.

Multiplexer—(see "film chain.")

Must Carry Signals—the Federal Communications Commission requires cable television systems to carry certain full-power television stations. All full-power stations within a certain mileage range, market area, and grade of signal (quality) are "must carries" for the cable operator. (Low-power television stations—LPTV—are not "must carries.")

NAB—an acronym for *National Association of*

Broadcasters, a major trade organization for broadcasters.

Narrowcasting—a cable program or service designed to appeal to a special interest group or standard demographic target rather than a broad segment of the population. Cable television features much narrowcasting, both in single programs and entire networks.

NCTA—an acronym for National Cable Television Associaton, the major trade association of the cable industry.

Network—(1) in video, a linking together of stations, cable systems or other entities by microwave, satellite, telephone lines, coaxial cable, or other delivery systems to receive programming from a central distribution or production point. (Networking is not limited to home viewing of television programs. A number of religious denominations have created networks for transmitting educational and other material to churches and integral organizations. Baptist Telecommunication Network (BTN) is one example. Another example is the Louisiana Interchurch Conference, a producer of pastor helps which have been delivered weekly to clergy of many denominations via satellite.) (2) In computers, an interconnection of computers and terminals, often with a common data base.

Ni-Cad—an abbreviation for nickle-cadmium, a type of rechargeable battery.

Nielsen—the A. C. Nielsen Company is a research firm which gathers data on television audiences for stations, networks, and cable systems.

Noise—an unwanted audio or video signal that interferes with the normal signal.

Nonfatal Error—a mistake in a computer program which still allows the program to progress.

Nonvolatile—computer memory which is not lost when the power is turned off.

NTSC—an acronym for National Television Standards Committee, an engineering advisory group to the Federal Communications Commission which recommends television standards. The current NTSC practice is based on a 525-line/60-field system.

Omnidirectional Mike—a microphone with a pickup pattern which is equally sensitive to sounds coming from any direction.

On-Line—a computer term meaning a piece of equipment when it is working in conjunction with the computer's processor. A printer which is producing a data printout from the processor is "on-line." If the printer is also a typewriter and is switched over for independent use as a typewriter, it is "off-line."

On-Location—video productions made outside of a studio setting.

Open Mike—a microphone which is on.

Open Reel—magnetic audio and videotape systems that utilize separate feed and take-up reels, as opposed to cassettes which enclose both reels in a case or cartridge.

Orbital Position—the assigned location for a geostationary communications satellite above the equator.

Pacing—the overall rhythm of a program. Pacing determines how an audience perceives the time of segments and the entire program.

PAL—an acronym for Phase Alteration by Line, the standard color television system used by many European countries, Australia, and others. It is based on a 625-line/50-field system and is not compatible with the American NTSC 525-line/60-field system standard.

Pan—the direction given for horizontally turning a video camera to the left or right, such as to "pan left" or "pan right."

Parabolic Antenna (Dish)—the dish-shaped device for gathering microwave signals from a satellite and focusing them to one central point in front of the dish: the focal point. These antennas may be made of solid metal, metal mesh, fiberglass-coated metallic cloth, or even wood covered with a metal reflecting surface.

Parabolic Mike—a microphone mounted in a dish-shaped reflector, designed to pick up distant sounds. For example, networks use parabolic microphones on the sidelines at football games to pick up audio on the field.

PASCAL—a high-level computer language.

Pay-Per-View—an increasingly popular television option which allows viewers to pay for viewing a particular event such as a university football game. The viewer is given a special decoder to receive the program. If the decoder already in the home is addressable (see "addres-

Appendix I: A Video Glossary

sability"), the cable company activates it from the cable headend.

Penetration—the percentage of households subscribing to cable television in a coverage area. This is also referred to as "saturation."

Peripherals—computer devices which are not part of the computer's processor, such as printers, disk drives, and plotters.

Pickup Pattern—refers to the directions to which a microphone is designed to be sensitive to sound waves. One of the chief determinants for choosing a microphone is the pickup pattern which meets the particular need of a recording session. The three most common pickup patterns are: omnidirectional, unidirectional, and cardioid.

Pickup Tube—the vacuum tube in a videocamera which senses or "picks up" reflected light from a subject being shot and converts it to electric signals.

Picture Tube—a cathode-ray tube (CRT) which displays a video signal or picture.

Pirating—(1) copying/reproducing copyrighted materials (including videotapes) for sale without a license from the copyright holder; (2) receiving pay television without making payment.

Pixels (Picture Cells)—the thousands of dots which make up a television picture on a regular television set or monitor. Pixels are taken into account when producing graphics on a computer monitor screen.

Playback—the reproduction of sound or video from a recording.

Playback Head—an audio or video assembly which senses magnetic energy stored on tape or disc and converts it to an electric signal for processing into audio or video.

Plotter—a computer output device which produces pictorial data with the use of pens controlled by motors.

Plumbicon—a type of video pickup tube used in some cameras. Developed by N. V. Phillips, the tube is more sensitive than vidicon tubes.

Polar Mount—a type of satellite-receiving antenna (dish) mount that allows full access to the geostationary orbit belt of communications satellites above the equator through rotation on only one axis. Changes between satellites may be done with a hand crank or a motorized tracking system.

Polarity Rotator (Rotor System)—the device on a satellite-receiving system which selects the polarization, either horizontal or vertical. Some rotators change polarity by being physically moved by a motor. Other rotators change electronically. The rotator is attached to the feedhorn/LNA assembly.

Polarization—a term referring to the plane on which satellite signals are transmitted, either horizontally or vertically polarized. By using polarized signals, a satellite with twelve channels can double to twenty-four channels by transmitting two signals on each frequency but with opposite polarization.

Port—an outlet for a peripheral to plug into a computer's processor. (See *Peripherals*.)

Portapak—the name given to a portable, battery-operated video system of camera and recorder.

Postproduction—the final stage of the production process in which a videotape is edited, and the desired audio is included on the sound track.

Power Divider—a signal splitter for use on satellite-receiving systems to allow for receiving more than one channel at a time from a communications satellite. Multiple receivers are required, too.

Powerpack—a portable power supply which uses a rechargeable battery or batteries.

Preproduction Planning—the initial stage in which a program is designed and coordinated. (Preproduction meetings save hours of time and money as actual production begins.)

Preroll—(1) starting a videotape earlier than it is needed to permit it to attain proper operating speed and achieve stability; (2) the amount of time for a video recorder to run before a picture actually appears on a television screen or monitor.

Primary Colors—(1) the principal spectrum colors from which other colors are produced; (2) the three colors used in television: red, blue, and green.

Prime Focus—the most common type of satellite receiving system which has a feedhorn/low noise amplifier (LNA) assembly located in front of the dish antenna at the focal point (where microwave signals from the satellite bounce off the dish and concentrate).

Prime Time—the most watched hours of television, 8:00-11:00 PM (Eastern time).

Printer—an output device which reproduces data from a computer processor onto paper. Some printers can only print letters and numerals while others are capable of graphics.

Prism Optics—an optical system in three-tube color cameras which splits incoming light into red, green, and blue segments for pickup by the red, green, and blue tubes. Prism optics are to be found in most high-quality cameras.

Proc Amp—an acronym for *processing amp*lifier, a device for correcting video levels and synchronization pulses prior to broadcasting or cablecasting.

Process—in computers, a verb meaning to work on data in accord with instructions given.

Processor—the heart of the computer system which combines memory and a microprocessor to handle data (input and output) and to control the peripherals.

Producer—the team member who is responsible for the entire video or audio production.

Production—the third stage in producing a program, when sound and picture are actually broadcast live or recorded onto tape.

Production Music—music which is written and recorded for use as background or theme music for programs. For some production music, payment is required for each usage. (This is called a "needle drop" fee.) Other production music is of the "buy out" variety. This music is for unlimited usage over a certain period of time or, in some cases, until the record or tape wears out.)

Program—(1) in computers, a set of instructions to cause the computer to perform tasks, such as problem solving; (2) in video, a production.

PROM—an acronym for *P*rogrammable *R*ead *O*nly *M*emory, a computer memory which can be permanently programmed by the user, not subject to erasure.

Protection—(1) full-power television broadcasts and other communications are "protected" by the Federal Communications Commission from interference by other broadcast transmissions. While full-power television stations are protected from interference by low-power stations (LPTV), low-power stations are not necessarily protected from interference by full-power stations. (2) Satellite receiving antennas (dishes) used by full- and low-power television stations as well as cable systems to receive program sources may be licensed (protected) by the FCC if they meet certain size and performance standards. (See "site survey.")

Public Access—a local cable television channel set aside for programming for and by the community. Generally, there are no stipulations on content, and use is open to the public on a first-come, first-serve basis.

Quartz Lighting—a type of lamp which provides high intensity illumination with a constant color temperature, also known as "tungsten-halogen" lighting. Quartz lighting is widely used in video production.

RAM—an acronym for *R*andom *A*ccess *M*emory, a computer memory that can be added to by the user but which disappears when the power is turned off.

Random Access—(1) in computers, it refers to items in memory which can be quickly accessed regardless of location in the memory; (2) in video, simple retrieval of the information, regardless of its location on a tape or disc, often computer assisted.

Raster—the illuminated area of a picture tube which is scanned by an electron beam. (See "How Video Works" for an explanation.)

Rating—a measure of television viewership. It is the percentage of all television households or all people in a certain demographic group who are watching a specific program or station.

Read—the process of transferring computer data from one storage device to another such as a disk or tape. Data is read from a tape, disk, or memory.

Real Time—actual time. A program done in real time has not been edited.

Receiver—(1) in satellite television, the component of a satellite-receiving system which converts higher microwave frequencies to lower frequency ranges usable on a television set. These receivers are capable of receiving twenty-four video channels per satellite and several additional audio channels. (2) In video, a regular television set as opposed to a monitor, which only receives a component video signal since it has no tuner.

Registered TVRO—if a satellite-receiving system (earth station or TVRO) is of sufficient quality and size, it can be registered and protected from terrestrial interference. A frequency-coordination study proving that no interference exists at the time of installation of the TVRO must accompany the registration request.

Registration—adjusting the three pickup tubes of a color video camera so that pictures they form are exactly superimposed upon one another.

Remote—a television program originating away from the studio.

Resolution—a method of defining video picture clarity or sharpness of detail. The greater the resolution, the greater the clarity of picture.

Retrofitting—rebuilding sections of a cable system or adding additional equipment, often to increase channel capacity or provide for interactive cable.

RF—an acronym for *Radio Frequency*, usually refers to television channel frequencies.

RF Modulator—converts signals from a video recorder, satellite receiver, computer, or other equipment into a form which can be received on a regular television set.

RG 59—another name for coaxial cable, (1) used by cable companies to connect homes to the system; (2) used for connecting various video equipment components.

Roll—(1) the movement of information vertically on the television screen, usually bottom to top. When credits are shown at the conclusion of a program, they are "rolled." (2) Lack of vertical synchronization which causes the picture to continually move up or down.

Rolling—in video, an indication that the recorder has been started and the tape is moving or "rolling."

ROM—an acronym for *Read Only Memory*, a computer memory which cannot be added to and which does not disappear when the power is turned off.

Rough Cut—a preliminary edit of a video program, subject to change.

Run—the command given to a computer to carry out the instructions of a program. "Load" is given before "run."

Running Time—length of a taped program or performance.

Runthrough—a rehearsal without interruption.

Satellite—a human-produced object or vehicle which orbits the earth, receiving transmissions and retransmitting them.

Saturation—(1) the vividness of color in a television picture; the richer the color, the greater the saturation; (2) The percentage of cable subscribers in relation to the homes passed by cable.

Scanning—the process of an electron beam tracing a pattern over the target area of a camera pickup tube to convert the light energy of each dot (pixel) into a corresponding electric signal. The process is reversed in producing a television picture by an electron beam "distributing" the same pattern on the picture tube raster. (See "raster.")

Scene—each location or setting in a video production which features some form of continuous action.

Scrim—(1) screen material placed in front of a light to decrease its intensity; (2) Cloth used in productions which appears opaque when lit from the front and transparent when objects behind it are lit.

SECAM—an acronym for *Sequential Couleur a' Memoire*, the standard color television system developed in France, based on a 625-line/50-field system. It is used in France, most of the Communist-bloc countries, and parts of Africa.

Secondary Storage—a computer term for data storage beyond the RAM and ROM capability of the computer. Disks and cassettes provide secondary storage capability.

Share—the percentage of homes using television which are tuned to a particular station at a certain time. Networks and local stations speak of "audience share."

Shot—an individual scene of a video production.

Shot List—a listing of shots to be made by a cameraman. This list is drawn from the script.

Shotgun Mike—a highly sensitive, unidirectional microphone used to pick up sound at great distances. The housing is long and slender.

Signal Splitter—a device which divides RF signals to supply more than one television set or recorder.

Signal-to-Noise Ratio—a measure of the relative strength of the desired signal to that of the background noise. A poor signal-to-noise ratio results in static in radio, "snow" in a television picture, and sparklies in a satellite television picture.

Site Survey—a study to determine the feasibility of a specific location for a satellite-receiving system. Included in the study is a microwave interference and terrain analysis.

Skew Control—an adjustment on some video recorders for correcting improper tape tension in the playback mode. Skew problems appear as curves or curved images at the top of the television picture when a tape is being played.

Slow-Scan Television—transmission of still pictures at a slow rate by using telephone lines or other communications channels with limited capacity. Slow-scan is a more economical way of handling teleconferencing or graphics transmission than full-broadcast video.

SMPTE Time Code—a code developed by the *S*ociety of *M*otion *P*icture and *T*elevision *E*ngineers to identify every video frame by hour, minute, second, and frame number for making precision edits.

Snake—a cable containing numerous individual lines with connectors on each end. "Snakes" are widely used for running audio circuits.

Snow—random picture noise on a television screen, possibly denoting a poor signal or dirty video heads.

Software—(1) in computers, the programs and accompanying materials which make the computer system work (see "hardware"); (2) in video, videotapes, videodiscs, and other expendable material.

Source Player—in editing or dubbing video material, this is the unit playing the prerecorded tape for pickup by the other unit. The source player is sometimes called the "master unit." The second unit is called "target recorder" or "slave unit."

Sparklies—small dots in a picture from a satellite-receiving system, indicating insufficient signal strength is reaching the receiver. Possible causes are a dish which is too small, imperfectly shaped, or not aimed properly.

Special Effects Generator (SEG)—a device for providing video effects in a program such as wipes, split-screens, and inserts. Computer-assisted equipment is also available for more elaborate effects.

Split Screen—a video special effect of two or more scenes on the television screen at one time, produced with a special effects generator by using two or more video sources such as cameras or recorders.

Spot—a television commercial.

Still Frame—freezing a single video frame on the screen.

Storyboard—a planning/production tool for video. Rough sketches of proposed scenes, camera instructions, and dialogue are placed on individual cards or sheets. These cards or sheets are for production personnel and help communicate what the director is trying to accomplish visually and aurally.

Subject—the focus of attention in a scene being videotaped.

Super—superimposing copy on a television screen. One example is a merchant "supering" his local logo or company name and address onto a national commercial playing in his television market.

Superstation—an independent television station which transmits its signal via satellite, thus making it possible to be received nationwide by cable systems and individual owners of satellite dishes. Atlanta's WTBS is a pioneer superstation.

Switcher—a device enabling an operator to select video signals from two or more sources.

Sync—an abbreviation for "synchronization" and "synchronizing." Sync signals are timing pulses that drive and coordinate the television scanning system, helping all related equipment to remain in phase with one another.

Sync Signal Generator (SSG)—a device for producing the sync pulses necessary to integrate various pieces of video equipment.

Tag—audio and/or visual information added locally to a commercial. For instance, a merchant might add information about local availability of a product on a nationally produced commercial. Such a commercial is "tagged."

Talent—the name given to all individuals who appear on camera.

Tally—a light on a video camera indicating that actions are being videotaped by that particular unit. Tally lights are useful when multiple cameras are being employed in a production.

Target Area—that portion of a video camera pickup tube which is light-sensitive. An electron scanning beam "reads" the image formed as light energy is focused on the tube by a camera's lens.

Telecine—(see "film chain.")

Telecommunications—the art of transmitting video, audio, and data via satellite, microwave distribution, local cable, or telephone lines to selected sites.

Teleconferencing—a form of telecommunications in which those receiving transmitted information are able to respond by telephone lines, two-way cable, microwave system, or satellite. Response may be by video, audio, or simple data transfer. Computers are also used in some teleconferencing exchanges.

TelePrompter—a brand name for a mechanical device which projects copy in front of a video camera lens for the talent to read.

Teletext—"pages" of textual information transmitted to a television set by broadcast or cablecaster. With an in-home adapter, viewers retrieve this information which is seen as letters and numerals on the screen. A few common applications of teletext are for news, financial information, weather, advertising, and so forth. Teletext technology can also make available research data from reference volumes such as encyclopedias and from other data banks.

Television Household—any household in which there is a television set. Growth of cable television is charted by comparing the number of television households, the number of households passed by cable, and the number of households subscribing to cable.

Television Receiver—an ordinary television set.

Terminal—any computer device which has input and output capabilities.

Test Tone—an audio tone produced by a tone generator and used as a reference in adjusting sound levels during recording and playback.

Theft of Service—(see "pirating.")

Tiering—the process of grouping cable program services available to subscribers. If subscribers desire more program services than those included in the basic monthly fee, they may subscribe to one or more tiers. Among services frequently found on tiers are movie and sports channels.

Tilt—the act of pivoting a video camera up or down on a tripod head. "Up" or "down" is based on the direction which the camera lens moves. Commands are "tilt up" or "tilt down."

Time-Sharing—a method whereby many computer users share a common CPU and data base.

Title Card—a graphic shot by a video camera.

Total Audience—the percentage of households which view some part of a program, not necessarily all of it. For instance, if 35 percent of all television viewers are watching a particular program, the program has 35 percent of the audience.

Track—an area on audio and videotapes which contains electronic video, audio, or control information.

Tracking Control—an adjustment on a video recorder which corrects distortion when tapes are played back on a different recorder than the type on which they were recorded. The distortion is caused by a variance in angle on which the video heads pass and "read" the tape.

Translator—a relay system for bringing distant or blocked-out television signals to an area. Signals are converted to a different channel frequency (to avoid interference) and retransmitted to an area where normal reception is difficult. Translators are quite common in mountainous regions.

Transmission—the sending of signals from one point to another.

Transponder—the portion of a communication satellite which receives signals from earth and transmits them back to earth. An average satellite has twelve to twenty-four transponders. Each transponder is capable of carrying one complete video signal plus several audio signals.

Tripod—a three-legged stand for mounting a camera.

Tripod Head—the top portion of a tripod where a camera is mounted. Different kinds of heads provide smoother movements for cameras than others. Fluid heads are usually more expensive but generally provide smoother operation than friction heads.

Truck—moving the dolly and video camera side to side (laterally). Commands are "truck left" or "truck right."

Trunk Line—the major distribution line for a cable system. It is not tapped for individual subscribers. Feeder lines branch off of trunk lines and are tapped to provide an individual "drop line" for serving a subscriber.

TVRO—an acronym for *TeleVision Receive Only*, an earth station (satellite receiving system) which magnifies a weak satellite signal into a video picture to be received on a television set or video recorder. Large TVROs produce a signal of sufficient quality to be broadcast or cablecast.

U-Format—the only 3/4" videocassette format. This format, also called "U-matic," gets its name from the "U-shaped" pattern by which the videotape wraps itself around the head drum when in the play or record mode. The 3/4" format was a failure as a home-recording unit when introduced in the 1970s. However, it revolutionized educational video and some broadcast and cablecast operations. Affordable videorecorders producing acceptable quality for stable duplication and many broadcasting/cablecasting applications were finally available with the introduction of the U-format.

UHF—an acronym for *Ultra-High Frequency*, regular television channels 14 through 83 on a television set (*not* cable channel frequencies 14 and above).

Unidirectional Mike—a microphone with a pickup pattern sensitive to sound coming from one limited direction, usually in front.

Uplink—a communications microwave signal from a transmitting earth station to a communications satellite. Most earth stations do not have the capability of transmitting, only receiving. Hence, they are called TVRO's—*TeleVision Receive Only*. Transmitting earth stations are large, quite costly, and require skilled operators.

Upstream—a signal traveling from a subscriber back to the cable headend.

User-Friendly—computer hardware or software which is easy to use.

VCR—an acronym for *videocassette recorder*, an electromechanical device for storing television sound and pictures on magnetic tape and playing them back on demand.

Vectorscope—a video test instrument for monitoring color reproduction.

Vertical Blanking Interval—the thick band separating video signals which can be seen on a television picture if it "rolls." This interval is produced during the scanning process at the beginning of each field. Some of these intervals can be used for carrying teletext as well as captioning.

VHF—an acronym for *Very High Frequency*, channels 2 through 13 on a regular television set.

VHS—an acronym for *Video Home System*, a 1/2" videocassette format developed by JVC for industrial and consumer use. VHS is a distribution format for much educational video and video movie rentals for homes. (VHS should not be confused with the other 1/2" format, Beta. VHS is the more popular format.)

Video—(1) the picture portion of a television broadcast; (2) an electronic signal carrying picture information.

Video In—(1) an input jack which delivers a video signal to a piece of equipment; (2) an input receptacle which receives a video signal.

Video Out—(1) the output jack which carries a video signal from one particular piece of equipment; (2) an output receptacle which delivers a video signal.

Videocassette—a given length of videotape on two reels in a cartridge or shell. This configuration aids in automatic threading.

Videodisc Player—a device for playing back prerecorded video programming which is stored on special flat discs. (See "laserdiscs.")

Videotex—(see "teletext.")

Vidicon—a type of color video camera pickup

tube developed by RCA. It is widely used in home video cameras.

Viewfinder—an electronic or optical device which permits a video camera operator to view the scene being shot. An electronic viewfinder is a television tube and, therefore, allows for viewing of material after recording. In other words, the viewfinder becomes a small monitor. An optical viewfinder is merely a hole in a camera body through which the operator sees approximately what the camera lens "sees."

Voice-Over—narration on a videotape where the speaker is not seen.

Volatile—memory which is lost when power is turned off to a computer.

VTR—an acronym for *vid*eo*t*ape *r*ecorder or *vid*eo*t*ape *r*ecording.

Waveform Monitor—a video test instrument for evaluating video signals, including the levels.

White Balance—an adjustment of red, green, and blue channels on a camera to produce the proper balance—white. Once the camera is "told" what white "looks like," it makes adjustment for all colors.

Wide Screen—a large-screen television set, either front or rear projection.

Wind Loading—the force exerted on a satellite receiving system and its supports by air pressure. Dishes should be able to withstand 120 mile-per-hour winds and sustain 40 mile-per-hour winds without interfering with the picture.

Wipe—a video picture transition from one scene to another in which the new scene is revealed by a moving line or pattern.

Wireless Microphone—a microphone using a radio transmitter and receiver, thus eliminating a connecting wire.

Write—to record computer data in a storage device.

Zoom—(1) a lens with a variable focal length; (2) the process of adjusting the lens.

Zoom Shot—shooting a scene with a steady, continuous adjustment of the camera's zoom lens from wide angle to telephoto or vice versa.